BETTER THAN THE BEGINNING:

Creation in Biblical Perspective

Richard C. Barcellos, Ph.D.

RBAP

Palmdale, CA

Requests for information should be sent to:

RBAP
349 Sunrise Terrace
Palmdale, CA 93551
rb@rbap.net
www.rbap.net

Printed in the United States of America.

Cover design by Kalós Grafx Studios | www.kalosgrafx.com

Formatted for print by Dean Thornquist.

ISBN 978-0-9802179-9-5

Creation is controversial, and truly we need to defend biblical doctrine concerning the origin of all things. Yet sometimes in the midst of controversy we can lose sight of the purpose of creation itself. Richard Barcellos uses the creation of the world like a great telescope to look up at the beauty of the Creator. His book focuses our attention on the triune God in Christ. He draws his doctrine from a careful exposition of the Bible, applies it to our practical lives, and calls us to sing the praises of Him who is worthy, "for thou hast created all things, and for thy pleasure they are and were created" (Rev. 4:11). This is an edifying book, and I hope that many will read it.

Joel R. Beeke, Ph.D.
President of Puritan Reformed Theological Seminary
Grand Rapids, MI
****

Although many Christians have been engaged in a life-or-death battle to defend the truth of creation against evolutionary attacks coming from inside and outside the church, there has been little exploration of the doctrine of creation in all its glorious height, depth, width, and length. Richard Barcellos has begun to remedy this neglect with a God-glorifying, soul-edifying, life-transforming survey of this majestic and practical subject.

David P. Murray, Ph.D.
Puritan Reformed Theological Seminary
Grand Rapids, MI
****

After reading this book, I wonder, 'is it possible that we are functional deists?' Have we been so profoundly influenced by the secular culture around us that we fail to see the centrality and foundational character of the doctrine of creation? Is it possible that even while giving lip-service to the doctrine we fail to live in the light of its implications? In this work, Dr. Barcellos shows us why this doctrine is so very important. Not only does he reflect upon the account of creation in Genesis, but he also demonstrates the implications of creation found throughout Scripture. In a day of increasing secularization, it is refreshing to think of the divine purpose in making and sustaining the world. Read this book, and you will deepen your understanding of the Lord's purposes in bringing the world into existence.

James M. Renihan, Ph.D.
Dean and Professor of Historical Theology
Institute of Reformed Baptist Studies
Escondido, CA
****

It is with special pleasure that I recommend both my friend, Richard Barcellos, and his volume entitled, *Better than the Beginning*. In a day of massive confusion about the significance God's relationship with Adam and departure from the pivotal Reformed understanding of the covenant of works, it is nothing short of refreshing to see both the heart for and insight into this subject that God has given Dr. Barcellos. While the New Perspective on Paul and other evangelical and "Reformed" scholars are manifesting deep insensitivity to Scripture on this subject, Richard provides clear and penetrating insight into God's purpose to bring the human race to a condition that is "better than the beginning." Christ brings the creation train derailed by Adam to its original glorious destination! This insight is vital to an understanding of the gospel and the vital, scriptural distinction between the law and the gospel. May God give this volume great usefulness!

Samuel E. Waldron, Ph.D.
Dean and Professor of Systematic Theology
Midwest Center for Theological Studies
Owensboro, KY
****

Table of Contents

Preface

This book started out as a series of sermons. After preaching a few installments of that series, I realized I was into a topic that was so vast I needed to cover more ground than originally intended. The series ended up comprised of over twenty sermons. In editing for publication, I tried to write as an author not as a preacher, though I do not think I succeeded. Because this book originated as sermons, it addresses both Christians and non-Christians on a very important subject relevant to everyone.

The reader who gets through the whole book will realize that, in one sense, this is not a typical book on creation. What I mean is that many books on creation deal with evolution, the length of the days of creation, and ethics in light of creation. These are worthy subjects and I do cover these things in this book. However, the doctrine of creation is much more inclusive in the Bible. Things that we think demand front-and-center attention do not get such by the Bible itself. As the title of the book seeks to display, the beginning is not the end of creation. Creation had a goal intended by God to be attained by man, but man failed. However, God will see to it that the original goal is reached. Creation, therefore, was intended to be a means to an end. The end is what God had in mind all along. The end is not plan B or even plan A. It is simply the plan.

Some explanation of the method I utilize in this book may help prior to reading. As the reader will see, I discuss the ultimate reason for creation, the divine agents of creation, the Son-tilted focus of creation, the revelatory function of creation, the initial act of creation, the six days of creation, the image-bearing apex of creation, and the Sabbath rest of creation. The approach I take is sometimes more textual or exegetical and sometimes more biblical-theological. The more textual or exegetical approach deals with one text or passage and its specific relevance to the topic under discussion. The more biblical-theological approach is a wider-lensed approach. Though it certainly deals with texts and passages, it also purposefully utilizes other biblical revelation to inform the study of the topic at hand in order to get the Bible's own interpretation or use of a given text, passage, or subject. There is a pattern in the Bible where later texts pick up on earlier texts. This gives us infallible interpretations or uses of those texts. These two approaches should not be seen as enemies or opposites. Within the interpretive process they are interdependent. Both are necessary and sometimes even indistinguishable.

I want to thank the congregation I serve, Grace Reformed Baptist Church, Palmdale, CA, for its support and encouragement. I especially want to thank the Lord for the time to study and think along with many of the great thinkers of the Christian church. I am not ashamed to admit that my work stands upon the shoulders of many others. Anything I say that is good and right is dependent upon the faithful teachers I have gleaned from over the years.

Richard C. Barcellos
Palmdale, CA
November 2012

Chapter 1

The Ultimate Reason for Creation:
Creation for the glory of God

Why? This is the question of the ages. Why this earth, the stars, and the moon? Why the sun, the planets, and the galaxy? Why the universe and why man? Why you? Why me? Why history? Where is history heading (if, indeed, it is heading someplace)? Who (if anyone) is driving this massive ship we call the universe which floats along at a pace we cannot alter and to which we are forced to submit?

Some say that everything exists because it just does. Matter, the things we can touch and feel, has always existed. That is just the way it is. If matter had a beginning, others say, it came from a variety of pre-existing things that worked together to form what we now call the universe. Everything that is, is because it just is. Billions and billions of years ago a system was put in place that, through various chance-happenings, ended-up producing you. You are the product of a series of impersonal, random, chance-occurrences. You are the result of a sort of primal, cosmic soup that happened to be stirred (by whom or what we know not) in such a way that you came as a result of it. There really is no meaning to life except that life forms are a part of an unstoppable process of change that may escort humans as we now know them off the stage of existence. This view of the universe is not very encouraging.

But is there a unifying principle (or better, a unifying Being), which gives understanding to the whole? Is there a One that provides an explanation for the existence of the many? Or are we left to try to interpret all these things with our puny brains which may remember today what they forget tomorrow without even remembering that they forgot something.

The Bible gives us a clear and simple, yet very astounding, answer to the question of why. Why are there galaxies, and stars, and the moon, and the sun, and planets, and the earth, and people, including you and me? The answer of the Bible is that the God who speaks to us through that which He has made and in His written Word, the Bible, made all things for His own glory. This answer to the question "Why?" is foundational to the rest of our study. It is not only foundational to our study, it is the key to interpreting everything that we see and know (including ourselves).

Exposition of Romans 11:36

In Romans 11:36, we read, "For from Him and through Him and to Him are all things. To Him *be* the glory forever. Amen."[1] This is a foundational verse in terms of understanding the Bible's teaching on the doctrine of creation. Paul's assertion implies that everything that is, is for "Him." This is crucial to understand. We will examine this verse under the following considerations: *The Context of Romans 11:36* and *The Content of Romans 11:36*.

The Context of Romans 11:36

Verse 36 is connected with verses 33-35 by the little word "For." Romans 11:33-35 says:

> [33] Oh, the depth of the riches both of the wisdom and knowledge of God! How unsearchable are His judgments and unfathomable His ways! [34] For WHO HAS KNOWN THE MIND OF THE LORD, OR WHO BECAME HIS COUNSELOR? [35] Or WHO HAS FIRST GIVEN TO HIM THAT IT MIGHT BE PAID BACK TO HIM AGAIN? (Rom. 11:33-35)

Verses 33-36 form a doxology, an anthem of praise, prompted by Paul's subject matter ending in verse 32, which says, "For God has shut up all in disobedience so that He may show mercy to all." The end of chapter 11 discusses the fact that God had delivered some

---

[1] English Bible references come from the New American Standard Bible unless otherwise noted.

first-century Jews to disobedience and was now showing mercy to Gentiles (11:32). Paul concludes this discussion with this bold assertion (11:32) and immediately follows with a sigh of wonder, astonishment, amazement, and praise (vv. 33-36).

The wider context of chapter 11 is dealing with God's sovereign display of mercy to non-Jews in the midst of wide-spread Jewish unbelief in Jesus as God's one and only Messiah–the only Savior of sinners. Romans 9-11 contain what we may call some of the hard sayings of Paul. He is dealing with the unbelief of God's ancient people in the first century. With sorrow and grief in his heart over his own people (Rom. 9:1-3), Paul deals with their wide-spread rejection of Christ. But the Christ they rejected is their only hope for salvation. This is why Paul is so grieved. In essence, though, Paul argues that God judicially hardens some while lavishing mercy upon others. Listen to what Paul says in Romans 9:15-24.

[15] For He says to Moses, "I WILL HAVE MERCY ON WHOM I HAVE MERCY, AND I WILL HAVE COMPASSION ON WHOM I HAVE COMPASSION." [16] So then it *does* not *depend* on the man who wills or the man who runs, but on God who has mercy. [17] For the Scripture says to Pharaoh, "FOR THIS VERY PURPOSE I RAISED YOU UP, TO DEMONSTRATE MY POWER IN YOU, AND THAT MY NAME MIGHT BE PROCLAIMED THROUGHOUT THE WHOLE EARTH." [18] So then He has mercy on whom He desires, and He hardens whom He desires. [19] You will say to me then, "Why does He still find fault? For who resists His will?" [20] On the contrary, who are you, O man, who answers back to God? The thing molded will not say to the molder, "Why did you make me like this," will it? [21] Or does not the potter have a right over the clay, to make from the same lump one vessel for honorable use and another for common use? [22] What if God, although willing to demonstrate His wrath and to make His power known, endured with much patience vessels of wrath prepared for destruction? [23] And *He did so* to make known the riches of His glory upon vessels of mercy, which He prepared beforehand for glory, [24] *even* us, whom He also called, not from among Jews only, but also from among Gentiles. (Rom. 9:15-24)

God may have mercy on whomever He pleases and whenever He pleases, and He cannot be impugned with evil because of it. He owes mercy to none. And when He shows it, He is simply being Himself, executing His divine and, therefore, sovereign prerogative. And for this, God should not be despised or argued with.

Romans 11:36 is the conclusion of Paul's doxology promoted by the unrivaled sovereignty of God in the with-holding and dispensing of mercy which displays the incomprehensibility of God's counsel (vv. 33-35).

The Content of Romans 11:36

Romans 11:36 reads, "For from Him and through Him and to Him are all things. To Him *be* the glory forever. Amen." Notice the connecting particle "For." This word connects verse 36 with verses 34-35. The questions in verses 34-35 are obviously rhetorical and the implied answer to each question is negative–no one. "For WHO HAS KNOWN THE MIND OF THE LORD, OR WHO BECAME HIS COUNSELOR? [35] Or WHO HAS FIRST GIVEN TO HIM THAT IT MIGHT BE PAID BACK TO HIM AGAIN? (Rom. 11:34-35). Verse 36 answers these questions: How come no one knows the mind of the LORD? How come no one has been His counselor? How come no one has first given to Him that it might be repaid to him? The answer is because "from Him and through Him and to Him are all things." In other words, no one tells God what to do. Man is not God's equal and certainly not His superior, not His advisor, nor counselor. Why not?

The three prepositional phrases of verse 36 are important to understand at this juncture. Here's an expanded translation of those phrases by Charles Hodge. "By Him all things are; through His power all things are directed and governed; and to Him, as their last end, all things tend."[2] Let us look at each of these phrases in order.

---

[2] Charles Hodge, *Romans* (Reprint 1989; Edinburgh and Carlisle, PA: The Banner of Truth Trust, 1835), 379.

The first one is "from Him ...are all things." God is the source, originator, and creator of all things. Many other places in the Bible affirm this same thing. Listen to three Scripture witnesses:

> In the beginning God created the heavens and the earth. (Gen. 1:1)

> [6] By the word of the LORD the heavens were made, And by the breath of His mouth all their host. [7] He gathers the waters of the sea together as a heap; He lays up the deeps in storehouses. [8] Let all the earth fear the LORD; Let all the inhabitants of the world stand in awe of Him. [9] For He spoke, and it was done; He commanded, and it stood fast. (Psa. 33:6-9)

> Worthy are You, our Lord and our God, to receive glory and honor and power; for You created all things, and because of Your will they existed, and were created. (Rev. 4:11)

Without any pre-existing materials to work with, without consulting architects, planning commissions, scientists, geologists, you or me, or anyone else, the God of the Bible spoke and the universe came into existence. That which became was not, until He said "Let there be" and suddenly, whatever He said to be, became and stands to this day. Everything that is, is because of Him.

How come no one knows the mind of the LORD? How come no one has been His counselor? How come no one has first given to Him that it might be repaid to him? Because God set things in order the way He wanted to because He possesses the right to. He's the potter and we're the clay (Rom. 9:20-21). He is first. He is primary. He is the Designer of all things and He needs no help, especially from such comparatively puny, weak, fickle, and sinful creatures as man.

The second prepositional phrase is "through Him ...are all things." God is the sustainer and providential ruler of all things. The Bible testifies of this truth in many places.

> All the inhabitants of the earth *are* reputed as nothing; He does according to His will in the army of heaven And *among* the

inhabitants of the earth. No one can restrain His hand Or say to Him, "What have You done?" (Dan. 4:35)

[6] That they may know from the rising of the sun to its setting That *there is* none besides Me. I *am* the LORD, and *there is* no other; [7] I form the light and create darkness, I make peace and create calamity; I, the LORD, do all these *things.* (Isa. 45:6-7)

In Him also we have obtained an inheritance, being predestined according to the purpose of Him who works all things according to the counsel of His will, (Eph. 1:11)

[27] "For truly against Your holy Servant Jesus, whom You anointed, both Herod and Pontius Pilate, with the Gentiles and the people of Israel, were gathered together [28] "to do whatever Your hand and Your purpose determined before to be done. (Acts 4:27-28)

[1] Praise the LORD! Praise the name of the LORD; Praise *Him,* O you servants of the LORD! [2] You who stand in the house of the LORD, In the courts of the house of our God, [3] Praise the LORD, for the LORD *is* good; Sing praises to His name, for *it is* pleasant. [4] For the LORD has chosen Jacob for Himself, Israel for His special treasure. [5] For I know that the LORD *is* great, And our Lord *is* above all gods. [6] Whatever the LORD pleases He does, In heaven and in earth, In the seas and in all deep places. [7] He causes the vapors to ascend from the ends of the earth; He makes lightning for the rain; He brings the wind out of His treasuries. [8] He destroyed the firstborn of Egypt, Both of man and beast. [9] He sent signs and wonders into the midst of you, O Egypt, Upon Pharaoh and all his servants. [10] He defeated many nations And slew mighty kings -- [11] Sihon king of the Amorites, Og king of Bashan, And all the kingdoms of Canaan -- [12] And gave their land *as* a heritage, A heritage to Israel His people. [13] Your name, O LORD, *endures* forever, Your fame, O LORD, throughout all generations. (Psa. 135:1-13)

We do not live in a closed system of reality. We are not off limits to the supernatural power and preservative care of the Almighty. God is no passive bystander. *Through* Him are all things. This is what theologians call divine providence. Richard A. Muller defines providence as follows:

> the continuing act of divine power, subsequent to the act of creation, by means of which God preserves all things in being, supports their actions, governs them according to his established order, and directs them toward their ordained ends.[3]

The extent of divine providence encompasses *all creatures* and *things*. This includes animate and inanimate things–men and animals, trees and mountains, stormy and sunny days, earthquakes and tsunamis, kings and queens, governments, traffic accidents, cancer and colds.

How come no one knows the mind of the LORD? How come no one has been His counselor? How come no one has first given to Him that it might be repaid to him? Because God not only *made* all things, He *preserves* all things, and He does so the way He wants to and often does things that we cannot understand. How can God make peace and create calamity (Isa. 45:7) and hold us accountable for our sin? How can the exhaustive, omni-comprehensive sovereignty of God and man's real, personal responsibility for evil be reconciled in our minds? They need not be and yet, they may both still be true. What matters, after all, is God's mind, not ours. Though we may not know how these things can both be true, He does.

The third phrase is "to Him are all things." All things redound to His glory, they reverberate His value, His worth, His beauty, and His majesty. Everything that is, is for Him. Again, the Bible is clear on this issue.

[89] Forever, O LORD, Your word is settled in heaven. [90] Your faithfulness *continues* throughout all generations; You established

---

[3] Richard A. Muller, *Dictionary of Latin and Greek Theological Terms* (Grand Rapids: Baker Book House, 1985, Second Printing, September 1986), 251.

the earth, and it stands. [91] They stand this day according to Your ordinances, For all things are Your servants. (Psa. 119:89-91)

The LORD has made everything for its own purpose, Even the wicked for the day of evil. (Prov. 16:4)

Everyone who is called by My name, And whom I have created for My glory, Whom I have formed, even whom I have made." (Isa. 43:7)

"For My own sake, for My own sake, I will act; For how can *My name* be profaned? And My glory I will not give to another. (Isa. 48:11)

To grant those who mourn *in* Zion, Giving them a garland instead of ashes, The oil of gladness instead of mourning, The mantle of praise instead of a spirit of fainting. So they will be called oaks of righteousness, The planting of the LORD, that He may be glorified. (Isa. 61:3)

[22] What if God, although willing to demonstrate His wrath and to make His power known, endured with much patience vessels of wrath prepared for destruction? [23] And *He did so* to make known the riches of His glory upon vessels of mercy, which He prepared beforehand for glory, [24] *even* us, whom He also called, not from among Jews only, but also from among Gentiles. (Rom. 9:22-24)

How come no one knows the mind of the LORD? How come no one has been His counselor? How come no one has first given to Him that it might be repaid to him? Because God has made all things and sustains all things for His glory and does not need to consult us concerning how to bring glory to Himself in what He does. God's supreme goal in all things, therefore, is His own glory, His own majesty on display, His own good, His own honor, His own value, His own praise, His own fame. God is in the business of fetching glory for Himself; He's in the business of self-advertisement. He regards Himself supremely. God created all things so that He would have a stage on which to display Himself. God takes supreme delight in making Himself known. Jonathan Edwards once said something like, "God delights in the expression of His perfections because they're His." Notice that he did not say, "God delights in the expression of His perfections because of their effect." Surely God delights in the effect of the expression of His perfections but He does that after the fact. Behind the expression of God's perfections is God's delight in those perfections themselves because they are His.

Notice the concluding ascription "to whom be glory forever." Paul cannot contain himself and basically says, "*soli Deo gloria!*" To God alone be the glory! Paul is ascribing to God what is due Him–honor, supreme value, praise, adoration and unrivaled worship.

Lastly, there is the final word, "Amen." What better way to end than to say, "So be it!"? Amen!

Implications of Romans 11:36

The universe is all about God, not man.

That should be clear by now. The vastness and mystery of the universe does not point to our importance, but to God's. The universe is a theater for God's glory. Living as if you are the center is the *problem* not the *solution*. Living for personal happiness is just that–personal. It is temporary. It does not last, nor does it satisfy the soul. It will bring you nothing but trouble when you face God at the great day of judgment. We are all restless and fickle until we find our rest in God and the only way to find your soul's rest in God is through Jesus Christ, the only Mediator between God and man. Come to Him for cleansing now, if you haven't. And if you have, thank Him, praise Him, adore Him. Why? "For from Him and through Him and to Him are all things. To Him *be* the glory forever. Amen" (Rom. 11:36).

When seeking to explain the purpose of the universe, the Christian, or biblical view, is to start with God, not man.

He is first and He gives meaning to all the rest. If we are trying to justify our belief in Christianity before an on-looking and unbelieving world, we should not assume it to be false or put it in a neutral category till proven true. If we truly believe Christianity has been revealed to man by God via the Scriptures of the Old and New Testaments, then we will tell others what the Scriptures say. The Bible does not need to be defended or proven by a litmus test outside of itself. As C. H. Spurgeon reportedly said, "The Bible is like a lion; just let it out of its cage and it will defend itself."

Deep theological questions that display our finiteness and creaturely limitations should move our souls to wonder and amazement.

Notice the first word of Romans 11:33, "Oh..." This is a word indicating astonishing adoration. This is the proper response to the doctrine of God's sovereignty in the withholding and dispensing of mercy. It is also the proper response to God's incomprehensibility. Whatever God ordains is right, simply because He ordained it. Though we cannot comprehend His ways, this is no grounds for not worshiping Him. In fact, it is just the opposite. The fact that God is merciful to anyone should astound us. He owes mercy to no one. Never forget this. But He does dispense mercy upon unworthy sinners. Those sinners go from rags to riches, children of wrath to children of God, enemies to friends, sons of Satan to sons of the Savior. These things should move our souls to praise and adoration.

The doctrine of the glory of God in all things affords great comfort for believers in Christ.

Knowing that God made all things, preserves all things, and directs all things to their ordained end, and all for His glory, is a marvelous comfort for believers in Christ. No matter what comes our way via divine providence, "we know that God causes all things to work together for good to those who love God, to those who are called according to *His* purpose" (Rom. 8:28). As hard, as difficult, and as gut-wrenching as the Christian life may be at times, the believer in

Christ may rest assured that God is "[o]ur shelter from the stormy blast."[4] William Cowper wrote a hymn in 1774 that embodies the doctrine contained in Romans 11:36. Read these words and let the truth of God's Word reflected in them sink deep into your soul.

1. God moves in a mysterious way His wonders to perform;
   He plants his foot-steps in the sea, And rides upon the storm.
2. Deep in unfathomable mines Of never-failing skill He treasures up his bright designs, And works his sovereign will.
3. Ye fearful saints, fresh courage take; The clouds ye so much dread
   Are big with mercy, and shall break In blessings on your head.
4. Judge not the Lord by feeble sense, But trust him for his grace;
   Behind a frowning providence He hides a smiling face.
5. His purposes will ripen fast, Unfolding every hour;
   The bud may have a bitter taste, But sweet will be the flower.
6. Blind unbelief is sure to err, And scan his work in vain;
   God is his own interpreter, And he will make it plain. Amen.[5]

This text answers the question "Why?"

That is a huge question and one all must face at some point. God made all things for His own glory. Let that sink into your soul. He is sovereign in all things, including the withholding and dispensing of mercy. The reason why we all need mercy is because we are sinners. We have all broken God's law. We are in a most pitiable state due to our sin. We are guilty and polluted, and we cannot change the state of our souls. We need God to look upon us with a pitiful eye, a merciful eye. He does just that through His Son, the Lord Jesus Christ. He sent Him to be the channel through which mercy gets from heaven to sinful souls on the earth. If you do not know God's mercy in Christ, if you know yourself as a guilty sinner, if you feel your need for a Savior, if you fear death (which I know you do

---

[4] Taken from the hymn "Our God, our Help in ages past" in *Trinity Hymnal: Baptist Edition* (Suwanee, GA: Great Commission Publications, Inc., 1995), hymn #26 (FIRST TUNE).

[5] *Trinity Hymnal*, hymn #21.

because God tells me so in His Word) and judgment and hell, I've got wonderful news for you. The day of grace is today. Today is the day to receive the mercy of God. Heaven is still in the business of dispensing mercy upon the needy, upon the helpless, upon the guilty. And heaven's mercy-dispenser is none other than our Lord Jesus Christ. His hands are full of pity joined with power to save. Turn from your sins to Christ. Turn to Him foul and filthy, come as you are. He is willing and able to save. If you do not know yourself to be a guilty sinner, if you do not feel your need for a Savior, if you do not think you fear death, and judgment, and hell, these things are sinful in themselves. Come to Christ with these sins as well, acknowledging them as such, and He will cleanse you.

Chapter 2

The Divine Agents of Creation:
Creation by the triune God

Understanding the Bible's teaching on creation is foundational to being able to give a defense to anyone who asks about the Christian's hope in Christ (1 Pet. 3:15). If we are going to defend our faith, we need to know what we are defending before we can defend it.

In the previous chapter, I attempted to show that the Bible teaches us that the ultimate reason why things are is for the glory of God. It was argued that "Everything that is, is for Him." "For from Him, and through Him, and to Him are all things. To Him be the glory forever. Amen" (Rom. 11:36).

This chapter asks the question, "Who is this God who created all things for His glory?" The answer is the triune God of the Bible–Father, Son, and Holy Spirit. This chapter will aim to prove to you that a Trinitarian doctrine of creation is taught in the Bible and foundational to the Christian faith, witness, and hope.

Defining our Terms

Using the terms "triune" and "Trinitarian" requires some explanation. That God is one is very clearly stated in the Bible. Deuteronomy 6:4 says, "The LORD is our God, the LORD is one!" First Corinthians 8:4 says, "...there is no God but one." However, historic Christianity claims that in one sense God is also three. For example, *The Baptist Catechism*, Q8, asks, "Are there more gods than one?"[1] The answer is "There is but one only, the living and true

---

[1] All references to The Baptist Catechism come from *The Baptist Confession of Faith & The Baptist Catechism* (Vestavia Hills, AL: Solid Ground Christian

God." Question 9 asks, "How many persons are there in the Godhead?" It answers, "There are three persons in the Godhead, the Father, the Son, and the Holy Spirit; and these three are one God, the same in essence, equal in power and glory." These kinds of questions and answers bring up other crucial questions. Let's explore some.

How can God be *one* and *three* at the same time? It all depends on what is meant by *one* and what is meant by *three*. *One* in what sense? And *three* in what sense? Is God *one* in every sense? No. Is God *three* in every sense? No. If the answer were yes to these questions, we would have an obvious contradiction. In fact, many throughout history and in our own day claim that the doctrine of the Trinity is a contradiction, even an absurdity. However, historic Christian orthodoxy has been extremely careful to qualify and define what it means by *one* and *three* as they relate to the doctrine of the Trinity. Careful definitions are extremely important while discussing this doctrinal formulation. Robert Shaw, for example, gives the following helpful explanation:

> We do not say that three are one in the same sense and in the same respect in which they are three; that would, no doubt, be a plain contradiction in terms. But we say, they are three in one respect, one in another respect–three in Person, one in essence; and there is no absurdity in that at all. It surpasses our reason, indeed, fully to understand it; and so do a thousand things besides, which yet we know are true and real. But, if it be a doctrine clearly revealed in the Sacred Scripture, we are bound to believe it, however incapable we may be of comprehending it.[2]

These distinctions between *one* (essence) and *three* (Persons) are vital to understand and can be borne out by Scripture, as I will attempt to show you.

Books and Carlisle, PA: Reformed Baptist Publications of the Association of Reformed Baptist Churches of America, 2010).

[2] Robert Shaw, *An Exposition of the Westminster Confession of Faith* (Geanies House, Fearn, Ross-shire, Great Britain: Christian Focus Publications, 1998), 72.

By *essence* is meant that which makes a thing or being what it is.[3] For example, "the essence of Peter, Paul, and John is their humanity; the essence of God is deity or divinity."[4] The essence of humanity is body/soul created in the image of God. Humans are creatures, created by God. They are dependent upon God for their existence. They are not eternal. The essence of deity or divinity, however, is uncreated, independent, self-existing spirit. God is an eternally self-existing spirit. Exodus 3:14 captures this well, "God said to Moses, "I AM WHO I AM"; and He said, "Thus you shall say to the sons of Israel, 'I AM has sent me to you.'"" We become; God simply is. We come into being. There was a time when we were not. God does not come into being. There was never a time when He was not. We are temporal. God is eternal. We depend on God for our existence. God is an eternally, independent, self-existing spirit. "God is spirit," Jesus said (John 4:24). Psalm 90:2 says, "Even from everlasting to everlasting, You are God." God is everlasting. He is eternal. The essence of God is independent, self-existing spirit. That's what constitutes Him as deity.

However, the Bible teaches that three Persons (i.e., the Father, the Son, and the Holy Spirit) share this one divine essence and, therefore, divine power and, as an expression of that divine power, the act of creation. In other words, this one divine essence is shared by three Persons and can be shown to be the case by what the Bible says about creation.

By *person* is meant an individual instance of a given essence.[5] The given essence, in this case, is deity or divinity. The three Persons are the Father, the Son, and the Holy Spirit.

The goal of this chapter is to show you that the one essence of God is possessed by three Persons who were actors in the drama of creation.

---

[3] Muller, *Dictionary*, 105-06.

[4] Muller, *Dictionary*, 105-06.

[5] Technically speaking, this definition of "person" is usually given for the word "subsistence." Subsistence is a more technical term used when discussing the Persons of the Godhead (cf. Muller, *Dictionary*, 290).

Three Persons yet One Essence

The Baptist Confession of Faith of 1689[6] has a wonderful statement reflecting the fact that three Persons share the one essence of God. It says:

> In this divine and infinite Being there are three subsistences,[7] the Father, the Word or Son, and Holy Spirit, of one substance, power, and eternity, each having the whole divine essence (BCF 1689, 3.3a)

There are at least three types of texts which indicate to us that three Persons share the one essence of divinity. There are texts which speak of the three Persons of the Godhead. There are texts which identify each Person as God. And there are texts which indicate each Person of the Godhead is eternal. Considered together, these texts indicate to us that the confessional formulation is an accurate reflection of what the Bible teaches.

Texts speaking of the three Persons

Here are three texts which speak of the three Persons of the Godhead.

> Come near to Me, listen to this: From the first I have not spoken in secret, From the time it took place, I was there. And now the Lord GOD has sent Me,[8] and His Spirit. (Isa. 48:16)

---

[6] All references to The Baptist Confession of Faith of 1689 come from *The Baptist Confession of Faith & The Baptist Catechism* (Vestavia Hills, AL: Solid Ground Christian Books and Carlisle, PA: Reformed Baptist Publications of the Association of Reformed Baptist Churches of America, 2010). This Confession will be abbreviated as BCF 1689.

[7] Remember, "subsistence" refers to an individual instance of a given essence.

[8] In the context of Isaiah, "Me" refers to the servant of the LORD, the Messiah to come, the incarnate Son of God.

[18] And Jesus came up and spoke to them, saying, "All authority has been given to Me in heaven and on earth. [19] "Go therefore and make disciples of all the nations, baptizing them in the name of the Father and the Son and the Holy Spirit, [20] teaching them to observe all that I commanded you; and lo, I am with you always, even to the end of the age." (Matt. 28:18-20)

The grace of the Lord Jesus Christ, and the love of God, and the fellowship of the Holy Spirit, be with you all. (2 Cor. 13:14)

Taken by themselves, these texts do not prove the doctrine of the Trinity. They do show us, however, that the Bible speaks of the Father, the Son, and the Holy Spirit together and sometimes in the same verse. As far as each Person being identified as God, other texts must be brought into the discussion (see below). But there is a pattern found in these texts of mentioning the Father, Son, and Holy Spirit which should pique the interest of the inquisitive Bible reader.

Texts which identify each Person as God

The Father is God. First Corinthians 8:6 is clear on this. It says, "yet for us there is *but* one God, the Father, from whom are all things and we *exist* for Him…" (1 Cor. 8:6). Here Paul is clearly identifying the Father as God.

The Son is God. Unlike 1 Corinthians 8:6, the texts which identify the Son as God have been the scene of various battlegrounds from time to time in church history. Though there are many texts which teach the deity of the Son, we will limit ourselves to two very clear ones–John 1:1 and Romans 9:5.

John 1:1 reads, "In the beginning was the Word, and the Word was with God, and the Word was God." The Word, later said to have become flesh (John 1:14), existed in the beginning (i.e., at the time of creation). John 1:3 goes on to say of the Word: "All things came into being through Him, and apart from Him nothing came into being that has come into being." This clearly implies that the Word never came into being. In other words, the Word was not created. There was never a time when He was not. John further asserts that "the Word was with God, and the Word was God." Two further things are asserted here of the Word: first, "the Word was with God;" and second, "the Word was God." In the first assertion, "the Word was with God," the Word and God are said to be in a relationship with each other and that relationship was already established "in the beginning." Relationship implies personality. The Word, therefore, is a distinct Person who "was with God." If this relationship of being "with God" implies the personality of the Word, then it also implies the personality of the one identified as God. But notice that John asserts that the Person identified as "the Word" is also said to be "God." What at first seems to be a contradiction is cleared up by recognizing that John is discussing the fact that "the Word" and "God" are both distinct Persons in relation to one another (i.e., "the Word was with God") and yet "the Word" shares the same essence as "God" (i.e., "the Word was God."). How can "the Word" be "with God" and "God" at the same time? The Word must be a divine Person in relation to another divine Person. This text clearly asserts that the Word, later identified as "the Light" (John 1:7, 8, 9), the One "coming into the world" (John 1:9), the One who "became flesh" (John 1:14), the One who "is in the bosom of the Father" (John 1:18), "the Christ" (John 1:20), "the LORD" (John 1:23), "Jesus" and "the Lamb of God" (John 1:29), and "the Son of God" (John 1:34) is God. Putting various texts together, John asserts that the Son is God.

Another clear text assigning deity to the Son is found in Romans 9:5. This text reads, "whose are the fathers, and from whom is the Christ according to the flesh, who is over all, God blessed forever. Amen." Elsewhere in the epistle to the Romans, Paul identifies Christ Jesus as God's Son (cf. Rom. 1:3). Romans 9:5 clearly refers to Jesus Christ, who is the Word who became flesh in John's language. Here, Paul asserts that "the Christ according to the flesh…is over all, God blessed forever." This is a textual witness to both the humanity and deity of the Son. The Christ is both "flesh" and "God blessed forever." Paul asserts that the Son is God.

The Spirit is also identified as God. Here is Acts 5:1-4.

But a man named Ananias, with his wife Sapphira, sold a piece of property, [2] and kept back *some* of the price for himself, with his wife's full knowledge, and bringing a portion of it, he laid it at the apostles' feet. [3] But Peter said, "Ananias, why has Satan filled your heart to lie to the Holy Spirit and to keep back *some* of the price of the land? [4] "While it remained *unsold*, did it not remain your own? And after it was sold, was it not under your control? Why is it that you have conceived this deed in your heart? You have not lied to men but to God." (Act 5:1-4)

The text implies the personality of the Holy Spirit (i.e., He could be lied to). But it also teaches that He is God. Peter said, "You have not lied to men but to God?" Who did Ananias lie to? He lied to the Holy Spirit. In lying to the Holy Spirit, Ananias lied to God.

The texts examined above identify the Father as God, the Son as God, and the Holy Spirit as God. There are three distinct Persons yet all identified as deity.

Texts which indicate that each Person is eternal

The Father is eternal. Psalm 90:2 says of the Lord, "Even from everlasting to everlasting, You are God." Since the Father is God (see 1 Cor. 8:6 referenced above), He is eternal. No one questions the eternality of the Father. But there are texts that teach the eternality of both the Son and the Holy Spirit as well.

The Son is eternal. Micah 5:2 says:

[2] "But as for you, Bethlehem Ephrathah, *Too* little to be among the clans of Judah, From you One will go forth for Me to be ruler in Israel. His goings forth are from long ago, From the days of eternity." (Mic. 5:2)

In the Gospel of Matthew, Micah 5:2 is applied to Jesus Christ (Matt. 2:5-6; cf. also John 7:42). Here eternality is ascribed to the Son.

John 8:58 is another text which implies the eternality of the Son. "Jesus said to them, 'Truly, truly, I say to you, before Abraham was born, I am'" (John 8:58). The words "I am" come from Exodus 3:14, which says, "God said to Moses, 'I AM WHO I AM'; and He said, "Thus you shall say to the sons of Israel, 'I AM has sent me to you.'" Notice the response by some who heard Jesus say this. "Therefore they picked up stones to throw at Him, but Jesus hid Himself and went out of the temple" (John 8:59). Jesus was ascribing deity to Himself. Claiming to be the "I am" is a claim to eternality. The great "I am" simply is; He never became. The Son is eternal.

There are at least two other texts which imply the eternality of the Son. Both John 1:3 and Colossians 1:16 ascribe the act of creation to the Word or Son of God. John even says that "apart from Him nothing came into being that has come into being" (John 1:3). This implies that the Word or Son pre-existed everything that has come into being and is not Himself part of that which came into being. Only God never came into being because He is eternal. The Son, being God, is eternal.

The Spirit is eternal. Hebrews 9:14 says, "how much more will the blood of Christ, who through the eternal Spirit offered Himself without blemish to God, cleanse your conscience from dead works to serve the living God?" Here eternality is ascribed to the Spirit who was identified as God in Acts 5 above.

The Bible teaches that three eternal Persons (i.e., the Father, Son, and Holy Spirit) called God share the one essence of deity. Each Person is identified as God and ascribed with eternality. Since only God is eternal, each Person is God. This is the doctrine of the Trinity. Listen to the Confession again:

> In this divine and infinite Being there are three subsistences, the
> Father, the Word or Son, and Holy Spirit, of one substance, power,
> and eternity, each having the whole divine essence (BCF 1689,
> 3.3a)

The Act of Creation and the Three Persons of the Godhead

We will look at two types of texts in this section. First, there are texts that attribute creation to the three Persons of the Godhead. Second, there are texts that attribute plurality to the Godhead at creation.

Texts that attribute creation to the three Persons of the Godhead

Hebrews 1:1-2 distinguishes between God (i.e., the Father) and His Son and attributes creation to God through His Son.

> [1] God, after He spoke long ago to the fathers in the prophets in many portions and in many ways, [2] in these last days has spoken to us in His Son, whom He appointed heir of all things, through whom also He made the world. (Heb. 1:1-2)

Hebrews 1:1-2 ascribes creation to the Father (and the Son).

Colossians 1:16 asserts that the Son created all things. "For by Him all things were created, *both* in the heavens and on earth, visible and invisible, whether thrones or dominions or rulers or authorities-- all things have been created through Him and for Him" (Col. 1:16). The "Him" of Colossians 1:16 is identified as the "Son" of Colossians 1:13. John 1:3 asserts the same. "All things came into being through Him, and apart from Him nothing came into being that has come into being" (John 1:3). These texts ascribe creation to the Son.

At least two texts indicate that the Spirit of God exerted divine, creative power. Genesis 1:2 says, "The earth was formless and void, and darkness was over the surface of the deep, and the Spirit of God was moving over the surface of the waters." Job 33:4 says, "The Spirit of God has made me, And the breath of the Almighty gives me life." Both of these texts attest to the Holy Spirit's activity in creation.

Holy Scripture attributes creation and, therefore, the power necessary for creation to the Father, Son, and Holy Spirit. Each Person in the Godhead possesses creative power and exerted the same in the beginning. Since creative power is attributed to God alone, each Person in the Godhead is *of one power*–divine power, as the Confession asserts.

Texts that attribute plurality to the Godhead at creation

Genesis 1:1 says, "In the beginning God created the heavens and the earth." The Hebrew word for "God" here is *Elohim*. It is a plural form of the word and is used this way throughout the Old Testament. There is a singular form of the word that Moses and the other Old Testament authors could have used–*Eloah*–but they did not.[9] Also, the verb "created" is singular. The first verse of the Bible, then, indicates plurality and "a diversity within the being of the One God who created all things."[10]

Then there's the witness of Genesis 1:26. "Then God said, 'Let Us make man in Our image, according to Our likeness; and let them rule over the fish of the sea and over the birds of the sky and over the cattle and over all the earth, and over every creeping thing that creeps on the earth" (Gen. 1:26). Again, plurality in the One who created is clearly asserted. Here we have what Douglas F. Kelly calls an executive divine counsel concerning the making of man.[11] What later becomes a clear revelation of the doctrine of the Trinity in the Bible is here given an implicit testimony.

Genesis 1:2 indicates that the Spirit of God was active at the creation and then in verse 3 the word of God commands things into existence. Genesis 1:2-3 says, "The earth was formless and void, and darkness was over the surface of the deep, and the Spirit of God

---

[9] See Douglas F. Kelly, *Systematic Theology, Volume One, Grounded in Holy Scripture and understood in the light of the Church, The God who is: the Holy Trinity* (Geanies House, Fearn, Ross-shire, Scotland, UK: Mentor, 2008), 456.

[10] Kelly, *Systematic Theology*, I:456.

[11] Douglas F. Kelly, *Creation and Change: Genesis 1.1-2.4 in the Light of Changing Scientific Paradigms* (Geanies House, Fearn, Ross-shire, Scotland, UK: Mentor, 1997, re. 2010), 193.

was moving over the surface of the waters. Then God said, "Let there be light"; and there was light." If we link this with John 1:1-3, then the word of God could be the pre-incarnate Son of God.

These texts are not as clear as the texts examined in the section on explicit examples of creation attributed to each Person in the Godhead. They should, however, be allowed a subordinate place in the overall formulation of our doctrine of the Trinity as it relates to creation. The Bible teaches that each Person of the Godhead exerted divine power at the creation of all things. In other words, the Creator-God of the beginning is Father, Son, and Holy Spirit.

Practical Considerations

The doctrine of the Trinity (in our case as it relates to creation) is very practical. Let us consider some ways this doctrine may be useful to the believer's soul.

For proper praise and adoration

The doctrine of the Trinity ought to promote praise and adoration. Sadly, the Confession is considered by some to be an antiquated, sterile document devoid of ethos. However, in one of its most technical sections, it asserts this about the doctrine of the Trinity: "which doctrine of the Trinity is the foundation of all our communion with God, and comfortable dependence on him" (BCF 1689, 3.3c). The famous hymn by Reginald Heber, "Holy, Holy, Holy!," says it well:

1. Holy, Holy, Holy, Lord God Almighty! Early in the morning our song shall rise to thee;
   Holy, Holy Holy! Merciful and Mighty! God in three Persons, blessed Trinity!
2. Holy, Holy, Holy! All the saints adore thee, Casting down their golden crowns around the glassy sea; Cherubim and seraphim falling down before thee, Who wert, and art, and ever-more shalt be.

3. Holy, Holy Holy! Though the darkness hide thee, Though the eye of sinful man thy glory may not see; Only thou art holy; there is none beside thee Perfect in power, in love, and purity.
4. Holy, Holy Holy! Lord God Almighty! All thy works shall praise thy Name, in earth and sky and sea; Holy, Holy, Holy! Merciful and Mighty! God in three Persons, blessed Trinity! Amen.[12]

For understanding the Bible's teaching on both creation and redemption

As we have seen above, the Bible contains a Trinitarian doctrine of creation. When God acted in creation, each Person of the Godhead exerted divine power. But the Bible teaches the same about redemption. As will be shown in subsequent chapters, the good creation of God was stained by sin. The God who took it upon Himself to create also took it upon Himself to redeem, to save, to rescue. Ephesians 1:3-14 shows that the same triune God who created is the One who redeemed.

[3] Blessed *be* the God and Father of our Lord Jesus Christ, who has blessed us with every spiritual blessing in the heavenly *places* in Christ, [4] just as He chose us in Him before the foundation of the world, that we would be holy and blameless before Him. In love [5] He predestined us to adoption as sons through Jesus Christ to Himself, according to the kind intention of His will, [6] to the praise of the glory of His grace, which He freely bestowed on us in the Beloved. [7] In Him we have redemption through His blood, the forgiveness of our trespasses, according to the riches of His grace [8] which He lavished on us. In all wisdom and insight [9] He made known to us the mystery of His will, according to His kind intention which He purposed in Him [10] with a view to an administration suitable to the fullness of the times, *that is*, the summing up of all things in Christ, things in the heavens and things on the earth. In Him [11] also we have obtained an inheritance, having been predestined according to His purpose who works all things after the counsel of His will, [12] to the end that

---

[12] *Trinity Hymnal*, hymn #87.

we who were the first to hope in Christ would be to the praise of His glory. [13] In Him, you also, after listening to the message of truth, the gospel of your salvation-- having also believed, you were sealed in Him with the Holy Spirit of promise, [14] who is given as a pledge of our inheritance, with a view to the redemption of *God's own* possession, to the praise of His glory. (Eph. 1:3-14)

The Father *planned* redemption (Eph. 1:3-6), the Son *accomplished* it (Eph. 1:7-12), and the Holy Spirit *applies* it (Eph. 1:13-14). As God acted in a Trinitarian fashion in creation, so He works the same in redemption. Second Corinthians 4:6 says, "For God, who said, 'Light shall shine out of darkness,' is the One who has shone in our hearts to give the Light of the knowledge of the glory of God in the face of Christ" (2 Cor. 4:6). There is an allusion here to Genesis 1:3, which says, "Then God said, 'Let there be light'; and there was light" (Gen. 1:3). This will become clearer as we develop the Bible's teaching on creation is subsequent chapters. For now, take note of the fact that creation and redemption motifs are vitally related. Hymn #88 of the *Trinity Hymnal* says it well:

1. Father of heaven, whose love profound A ransom for our soul hath found, Before thy throne we sinners bend; To us thy pardoning love extend.
2. Almighty Son, Incarnate Word, Our Prophet, Priest, Redeemer, Lord, Before thy throne we sinners bend; To us thy saving grace extend.
3. Eternal Spirit, by whose breath The soul is raised from sin and death, Before thy throne we sinners bend; To us thy quickening power extend.
4. Jehovah! Father, Spirit, Son, Mysterious Godhead, three in One, Before thy throne we sinners bend; Grace, pardon, life to us extend. Amen.

For marveling at the incarnation of the Son

Hebrews 10:5 says, "...a body You have prepared for Me." This text indicates a wonderful truth related to both creation and redemption. The Father prepared a body (i.e., creation) for the Son to assume in order to accomplish His work (i.e., redemption). Galatians 4:4-6 adds:

> [4] But when the fullness of the time came, God sent forth His Son, born of a woman, born under the Law, [5] so that He might redeem those who were under the Law, that we might receive the adoption as sons. [6] Because you are sons, God has sent forth the Spirit of His Son into our hearts, crying, "Abba! Father!" (Gal. 4:4-6)

The Father sent the Son to become one of us to save us and give us the Spirit. The Father prepared a body for the Son to assume that believers might possess the Holy Spirit. The Son, who created all things, became what He was not in order that we might become what we were not. The Son of God became man for us and for our salvation.

For understanding the redemptive story-line of the Bible

The Bible's teaching on creation by the triune God is foundational to its redemptive story-line. This may be seen by the fact that the first words of the Bible are about creation–"In the beginning God created the heavens and the earth" (Gen. 1:1). But take notice of the end of the Bible–"Then I saw a new heaven and a new earth..." (Rev. 21:1). Between those two book-ends, we are told that the ground is cursed (Gen. 3:17) but we are also told that "...the creation itself also will be set free from its slavery to corruption into the freedom of the glory of the children of God" (Rom. 8:21). We are told that man has inherited a curse, but also that "There will no longer be any curse" (Rev. 22:3). And then, the central thrust of the Bible is about One who becomes a curse for others and whose work of redemption affects cursed humanity *and* the cursed creation. Christ became a curse for us (Gal. 3:13). We are told that "...if anyone is in Christ, he is a new creation..." (2 Cor. 5:17). Literally, it reads, "...if anyone is in Christ, new creation..." Peter tells us that when the Lord Jesus comes again, He will usher in "new heavens and a new earth" (2 Pet. 3:13). Christ becomes a curse and releases the cursed creation from its bondage. Creation and redemption are related to one another in the Bible.

Another text which illustrates the relationship between creation and redemption is Colossians 1:13-22.

> [13] For He rescued us from the domain of darkness, and transferred us to the kingdom of His beloved Son, [14] in whom we have redemption, the forgiveness of sins. [15] He is the image of the invisible God, the firstborn of all creation. [16] For by Him all things were created, *both* in the heavens and on earth, visible and invisible, whether thrones or dominions or rulers or authorities-- all things have been created through Him and for Him. [17] He is before all things, and in Him all things hold together. [18] He is also head of the body, the church; and He is the beginning, the firstborn from the dead, so that He Himself will come to have first place in everything. [19] For it was the *Father's* good pleasure for all the fullness to dwell in Him, [20] and through Him to reconcile all things to Himself, having made peace through the blood of His cross; through Him, *I say*, whether things on earth or things in heaven. [21] And although you were formerly alienated and hostile in mind, *engaged* in evil deeds, [22] yet He has now reconciled you in His fleshly body through death, in order to present you before Him holy and blameless and beyond reproach--
> (Col. 1:13-22)

Notice that Christ is both Creator of all things (Col. 1:16) and head of the church (Col. 1:18). Notice also that Christ reconciles all things (Col. 1:20). Sin brought a rupture to the cosmos. Sin brought distortion and curse. Mankind is fallen in sin and under a divine curse. Even some angels fell from their first abode (2 Pet. 2:4; Jude 6). It all seemed to go so wrong. God gave His first earthly son, Adam (Luke 3:38), the earth to subdue (Gen. 1:28) for His glory (Rom. 11:36). But Adam failed miserably. The last Adam, our Lord Jesus Christ (1 Cor. 15:45), however, will not fail. He will bring many sons to a glorified state of sinless perfection (Heb. 2:10), wherein all the glory, all the lauding, and all the honoring goes to Him, and rightly so.

So the Bible goes from an old creation by the triune God for His glory to a new creation (2 Cor. 5:17; 2 Pet. 3:13; Rev. 21:1). It goes from the old creation headed-up by the first Adam that was stained and infected by sin to a new creation headed-up by the last Adam (1 Cor. 15:45 and Eph. 1:10, 22-23), Christ Jesus. This new creation, unlike the first creation, will be absolutely and eternally impervious to sin (2 Pet. 3:13). The Bible's teaching on creation is pretty important if we are going to understand the Bible. And the Bible's teaching on creation does not end in Genesis 1 and 2.

The triune God–Father, Son and Holy Spirit–made all things for His own glory. *Soli Deo gloria!*

Chapter 3

The Son-Tilted Focus of Creation:
Creation for the Son of God

I have argued that creation exists for the glory of God–*soli Deo gloria* (Rom. 11:36)–and was an act of the triune God. This chapter will argue for the Son-tilted focus of creation. Our text for consideration is Colossians 1:16. It reads:

> For by Him all things were created, *both* in the heavens and on earth, visible and invisible, whether thrones or dominions or rulers or authorities--all things have been created through Him and for Him. (Col. 1:16)

In the creation of all things unto the glory of God by the triune God, there was particular focus aimed at the glory of the Son of God.

Context of Colossians 1:16

In order to understand this verse properly, understanding its context is essential. Notice that verse 16 is connected to what goes before it, indicated by the word "For." This verse is actually connected to Paul's prayer which he announces in 1:9. It will help to read the entire passage.

> [9] For this reason also, since the day we heard *of it*, we have not ceased to pray for you and to ask that you may be filled with the knowledge of His will in all spiritual wisdom and understanding, [10] so that you will walk in a manner worthy of the Lord, to please *Him* in all respects, bearing fruit in every good work and increasing in the knowledge of God; [11] strengthened with all power, according to His glorious might, for the attaining of all steadfastness and patience; joyously [12] giving thanks to the Father,

who has qualified us to share in the inheritance of the saints in Light. [13] For He rescued us from the domain of darkness, and transferred us to the kingdom of His beloved Son, [14] in whom we have redemption, the forgiveness of sins. [15] He is the image of the invisible God, the firstborn of all creation. [16] For by Him all things were created, *both* in the heavens and on earth, visible and invisible, whether thrones or dominions or rulers or authorities-- all things have been created through Him and for Him. (Col. 1:9-16)

In Colossians 1:9, Paul lets his readers know that he is praying for them: "For this reason also, since the day we heard *of it*, we have not ceased to pray for you and to ask that you may be filled with the knowledge of His will in all spiritual wisdom and understanding." In 1:10a he announces the goal of his prayer: "so that you will walk in a manner worthy of the Lord, to please *Him* in all respects." He wanted them to please God. In 1:10bff. Paul identifies what a life that pleases God looks like. A life that pleases God bears fruit in every good work (1:10b), "bearing fruit in every good work..." A life that pleases God increases in the knowledge of God (1:10c), "increasing in the knowledge of God..." A life that pleases God is a strengthened life (1:11a), "strengthened with all power..." And a life that pleases God gives thanks to the Father (1:11bff.), "joyously giving thanks to the Father..." Then Paul gives us three reasons for thanking the Father: (1) because He "has qualified us..." (1:12b), (2) because "He rescued us..." (1:13a), and (3) because "[He] transferred us to the kingdom of His beloved Son" (1:13b).

Having mentioned the Father's Son in 1:13, Paul describes Him as follows. First, He is the Father's "beloved" Son (1:13b). This refers to His relation to the love of the Father. Second, He is the One "in whom we have redemption" (1:14). This is the Son's relation to the Father's plan of salvation. Third, He is "the image of the invisible God" (1:15a). This is the Son's relation to the divine essence. And fourth, the Son is "the first-born of all creation" (1:15b). This is His relation to the creation. But what does this mean?

What does it mean that the Son is "the first-born of all creation"

(Col. 1:15b)? First let us consider what it does not mean. It does not mean the Son was the first created being. Paul does not say, "who is the first-created of all creation." The early church dealt with this long ago. Heretics were claiming that there was a time when the Son was not. In other words, they said the Son of God came into being like all other created things. But in John 1:1-3, discussed above, it is clear that the One who became flesh according to John 1:14 is the Word of John 1:1 who created all things according to John 1:3. "All things came into being through Him, and apart from Him nothing came into being that has come into being" (John 1:3). The Word never came into being. He brought things into being that had no being but never came into being Himself. The Son is not a created being. There was never a time the Son was not.

What does it mean that the Son is "the first-born of all creation" (Col. 1:15b)? It is important to study the Old Testament roots of the concept of the first-born. For instance, Psalm 89:27 says, "I also shall make him My firstborn, The highest of the kings of the earth." This Psalm deals with the Davidic covenant and applies ultimately to the Lord Jesus in His mediatorial role as David's royal or kingly son (See Acts 2:30 where Peter makes this connection.). The "first-born" king does not mean the first king ever to exist or the first king to come into being. It refers to preeminence, rank, and authority. It is of interest to note as well that ancient Israel is called both God's son and "firstborn" in Exodus 4:22. Yet the first son of God on the earth was Adam in the garden of Eden according to Luke 3:38. So the concept of firstborn does not refer to temporality. Being "the first-born of all creation" (Col. 1:15b) indicates that the Son is above creation. He ranks above and over it. He is its Lord, not its product. He is the acting President of the creation.

The concept of "the first-born of all creation" is crucial to understand Colossians 1:16 because the first word of that verse is "For," connecting it with verse 15.

Content of Colossians 1:16

Having established the context and flow of Paul's thought, we are prepared now to analyze the content of Colossians 1:16. We will do so under two considerations: first, its connection with 1:15 and second, its three prepositional phrases. Here is Colossians 1:16 again:

> For by Him all things were created, *both* in the heavens and on earth, visible and invisible, whether thrones or dominions or rulers or authorities--all things have been created through Him and for Him.

The connection of Colossians 1:16 with Colossians 1:15

First, notice the connection of verse 16 with verse 15 indicated by the word "For." This word introduces us to the reason why the Son is the first-born of all creation, why He is the preeminent One over all creation, why He is creation's Lord, not its product. The answer is given in three prepositional phrases.

Three reasons why the Son is preeminent over creation

The three reasons why the Son is preeminent over creation are borne out by three prepositional phrases: "...*by* Him...*through* Him...*for* Him" (emphasis mine). We will consider each in the order Paul gives them.

Paul says, "For by Him all things were created, *both* in the heavens and on earth, visible and invisible, whether thrones or dominions or rulers or authorities--..." The preposition "by" refers to authorship. The Son is the conceiver, the author, the designer of that which has been created.

Paul continues by saying, "all things have been created through Him" "Through" refers to agency. Through the exertion of the divine, creative power of the Son, all things were created.

Finally, Paul says, "and [all things have been created] for Him." "For" refers to goal, purpose, or end. Commenting on this text, John Eadie says:

It is not...the wise and tasteful arrangement of pre-existent materials or the reduction of chaos to order, beauty, and life, which is here ascribed to [the Son], but the summoning of universal nature into original existence. What had no being before was brought into being by Him. The universe was not till He commanded it to be... Every form of matter and life owes its origin to the Son of God, no matter in what sphere it may be found, or with what qualities it may be invested. "In heaven or on earth." Christ's creative work was no local or limited operation...its sweep [encompasses] the universe..."heaven and earth." Every form and kind of matter, simple or complex–the atom and the star, the sun and the clod–every grade of life from the worm to the angel–every order of intellect and being around and above us, the splendours of heaven and the nearer phenomena of earth, are the products of the First-born.[1]

[All that has been made] bow[s] to the Son of God as the ...author of [its] existence...[2]

Let no one say, He is an inferior agent–the universe was created "[by] Him;" let no one surmise, He is but a latent source–it is "[through] Him;" let no one look on Him as another's deputy–it is "for Him." In every sense He is the sovereign creator–His is the conception, and Himself the agent and end.[3]

This is high Christology, indeed. All that came into being came into being "by" the Son, "through" the Son, and "for" the Son. Everything that is, is for the Son of God to bring glory to the triune God. Creation is Son-tilted from the beginning.

Consequences of Colossians 1:16

There are many consequences of this assertion by the Apostle Paul. We will focus on ones that are immediately related to our subject matter–creation and its implications.

---

[1] John Eadie, *Colossians* (1980 reprint; Klock & Klock, 1856), 53.
[2] Eadie, *Colossians*, 55.
[3] Eadie, *Colossians*, 57.

The Son is God the Creator.

Paul's language is all-inclusive. The Son is the Creator of all things. "For by Him all things were created, *both* in the heavens and on earth, visible and invisible, whether thrones or dominions or rulers or authorities--all things have been created through Him and for Him" (Col. 1:16). The divine being that Moses speaks of in Genesis 1:1 includes the Son. The Word of John 1:1-3 is the Son of Colossians 1. The Son of God is the efficient cause of the creation of all things. And all that has been made has been made "for" Him.[4]

Creation is Son-tilted from the beginning.

Our text clearly teaches this, but there are hints of the same teaching elsewhere that at first sight might seem surprising. For example, in Romans 5:14, Paul says, "Nevertheless death reigned from Adam until Moses, even over those who had not sinned in the likeness of the offense of Adam, who is a type of Him who was to come." Here Paul views Adam as a type of Christ. Adam did not become a type of Christ when Paul penned these words. God stationed Adam at creation as a type of Him who was to come. Adam was a type of Christ prior to the entrance of sin. Creation is Son-tilted from the beginning.

   Another text which illustrates the Son-tilted focus of creation is Ephesians 5:31-32.

> [31] FOR THIS REASON A MAN SHALL LEAVE HIS FATHER AND MOTHER AND SHALL BE JOINED TO HIS WIFE, AND THE TWO SHALL BECOME ONE FLESH. [32] This mystery is great; but I am speaking with reference to Christ and the church. (Eph. 5:31-32)

Marriage, from the beginning, was a living picture of Christ and the church. Since Adam was a type of Christ, Eve could well be a type of the church–even prior to the entrance of sin. J. V. Fesko calls the

---

[4] Colossians 1:16 echoes Romans 11:36.

church "the second Eve."[5] Commentator Peter T. O'Brien says, "...it was God's intention from the beginning when he instituted marriage to picture the relationship between Christ and his redeemed people."[6]

Now let us tease this out a bit. If creation is Son-tilted from the beginning and is "for" Him, then providence (God's constant activity which guides creation to its goal via divine power and ordained means) will be Son-tilted. And if both creation and providence are Son-tilted, then would not redemption be Son-tilted as well? Paul's words in Colossians 1:17-20 seem to support this.

According to Colossians 1:17, we may assert that providence is Son-tilted. Speaking of the Son, "by" whom, "through" whom, and "for" whom all things exist (Col. 1:16), Paul says, "He is before all things, and in Him all things hold together" (Col. 1:17). That which depends on the Son for initial existence depends on the Son for continued existence. That which was created "for Him" is subsequently sustained "in Him" (i.e., in the sphere of His providential power). Eadie says, "All things were brought together, and are still held together"[7] by Him, through Him, and for Him. He who created is alone able to sustain every moment of providence. Eadie continues:

> His arm upholds the universe, and if it were withdrawn, all things would fade into their original non-existence. His great empire depends upon Him in all its provinces–life, mind, sensation, and matter; atoms beneath us to which geology has not descended, and stars beyond us to which astronomy has never penetrated. He feeds the sun with fuel, and vails the moon in beauty. He guides the planets on their journey, and keeps them from collision and disorder.[8]

---

[5] J. V. Fesko, *Last Things First: Unlocking Genesis 1-3 with the Christ of Eschatology* (Geanies House, Fearn, Ross-shire, Scotland: Christian Focus Publications, Mentor Imprint, 2007), 168.

[6] Quoted in Fesko, *Last Things First*, 168.

[7] Eadie, *Colossians*, 59.

[8] Eadie, *Colossians*, 59.

Indeed, as Eadie concludes, "Every pulsation of our hearts depends on His sovereign beneficence who feeds and clothes us."[9] Just as creation is Son-tilted from the beginning, so is providence.

But Paul does not stop there. Redemption is also Son-tilted. In Colossians 1:18-20, we read:

> [18] He is also head of the body, the church; and He is the beginning, the firstborn from the dead, so that He Himself will come to have first place in everything. [19] For it was the *Father's* good pleasure for all the fullness to dwell in Him, [20] and through Him to reconcile all things to Himself, having made peace through the blood of His cross; through Him, *I say*, whether things on earth or things in heaven. (Col. 1:18-20)

He who is head of creation is also head of redemption–the new creation. The Son's work of reconciliation affects both sinful men and the cursed creation itself (cf. Rom. 8:20-21). Just as creation and providence are Son-tilted, so is redemption, the work of new creation. Ephesians 1 supports this. Paul says:

> [10] with a view to an administration suitable to the fullness of the times, *that is*, the summing up of all things in Christ, things in the heavens and things on the earth. In Him [11] also we have obtained an inheritance, having been predestined according to His purpose who works all things after the counsel of His will (Eph. 1:10-11)

> [22] And He put all things in subjection under His feet, and gave Him as head over all things to the church, [23] which is His body, the fullness of Him who fills all in all. (Eph. 1:22-23)

Listen to John Owen, a great seventeenth-century English Puritan theologian and pastor, on the concept of the centrality of the Son in the old and new creations. He says:

---

[9] Eadie, *Colossians*, 60.

God in infinite wisdom ordered all things in the first creation, so as that the whole of that work might be subservient to the glory of his grace in the new creation of all by Jesus Christ.[10]

For Owen, everything is Christocentric–creation, providence, and redemption. Richard Daniels says this of Owen:

It is difficult to conceive of a more Christocentric view of the purpose of God in creation than this, which subjects the creation and history of the universe to the manifestation of the glory of God in its renovation by the Son.[11]

Creation is Son-tilted (Col. 1:16). Providence is Son-tilted (Col. 1:17). And grace or redemption or new creation is Son-tilted (Col. 1:18-20).

There is, however, something staggering to consider here. The Son who made all things for Himself, by whom all things came into existence, and in whom all things maintain their current form of existence "became flesh and dwelt among us..." (John 1:14). He was "born of a woman, born under the Law" (Gal. 4:4). He became what He was not, while never ceasing to be what He always was and ever shall be–"God blessed forever. Amen" (Rom. 9:5). He who hung the stars became one of us. He who called all things into being out of nothing and sustains all things by His divine power, was hated without cause, laughed at, scorned, framed, rushed through a mock trial, crucified, and died in His human nature. What condescension! What humiliation! He who made human nature assumed that which He created in order to suffer, die, and rise from the dead in order to exalt it to a status never attained by Adam.[12] After He died, He rose in power, in glory. He suffered then entered into His glory (Luke 24:26, 46). He will come again in glory. And He will bring many sons to glory (Heb. 2:10).

---

[10] Quoted in Richard W. Daniels, *The Christology of John Owen* (Grand Rapids: Reformation Heritage Books, 2004), 179.

[11] Daniels, *Christology*, 180.

[12] We will discuss this concept in more detail below.

Chapter 4

The Revelatory Function of Creation (I):
Creation tells of His glory

The southwest rim of the Antelope Valley in southern California where I live is comprised of mountains. Some are small. Others are quite large. At first sight, these might appear to be markers of the huge divide between the valley and the much-larger (population-wise) Los Angeles basin. But, if you were on Google Earth Live and the camera lens started to widen, you would slowly but surely be able to tell that these mountains, which hold snow in the winter and provide a demarcating change in topography year-round, are actually part of the southern California mountains, which are in southern California, which is, of course, in the great State of California, which is located on the west (or best) coast of the United States of America, which is located on the continent of North America, which is part of the Northern or Western Hemisphere (depending on whether you start at the North Pole or the Prime Meridian), which is located on planet earth, which is part of the Milky Way galaxy, which is one galaxy among the possibly billions and billions of galaxies in existence, which are all located within the vast expanse of existence we call the universe. Putting things like the San Gabriel Mountains (which compared to us are quite large) into their widest perspective makes us feel quite small and it should. The universe we live in is a vast, powerful, amazing, twenty-four hour per day loud, non-verbal sermon being preached to all that has been made. Among the many places the Bible tells us this is Psalm 19:1-6. This Psalm clearly teaches that creation tells of the glory of God. Here is Psalm 19:1-6.

> For the choir director. A Psalm of David. The heavens are telling of the glory of God; And their expanse is declaring the work of His hands. [2] Day to day pours forth speech, And night to night

reveals knowledge. [3] There is no speech, nor are there words; Their voice is not heard. [4] Their line has gone out through all the earth, And their utterances to the end of the world. In them He has placed a tent for the sun, [5] Which is as a bridegroom coming out of his chamber; It rejoices as a strong man to run his course. [6] Its rising is from one end of the heavens, And its circuit to the other end of them; And there is nothing hidden from its heat. (Psa. 19:1-6)

Structure of Psalm 19

There are two major sections to this Psalm. The first six verses, quoted above, reveal the attributes and functions of creation. Some have called creation the natural book of God. These verses describe for us the attributes (i.e., descriptions of what it is) and functions (i.e., descriptions of what it does) of creation in terms of its revelatory status. This is also called General Revelation. Verses 7-14 of the same Psalm reveal to us the attributes and functions of the special book of God (i.e., Special Revelation or Holy Scripture). Our discussion below concentrates on the natural book of God or the revelatory function of creation.

Exposition of Psalm 19:1-6

God speaks to us today in two ways. He speaks to us in the Bible, His written Word, in words. But God also speaks to us in and through what He has made, though not through words. In other words, God speaks to us verbally, in the Bible, and God speaks to us non-verbally, in creation, through that which has been made. Paul says in Romans 1:20, "For since the creation of the world His invisible attributes, His eternal power and divine nature, have been clearly seen, being understood through what has been made..." God's revelation of Himself in creation is there for all to see. It has been that way from the beginning and it will never change. But the sky does not speak to us in an audible voice. We do not hear clouds talk. Stars do not converse with us. What can we learn from the vast sky above us? What can we learn from creation? Psalm 19:1-6 tells us.

The general statement concerning God's natural book

David identifies God's natural book in the first verse. He says, "The heavens are telling of the glory of God; And their expanse is declaring the work of His hands" (Psa. 19:1). "The heavens" refers to the things in the sky–the upper regions or the visible heaven or the celestial (from Latin, *caelum*) world, as opposed to this terrestrial (from Latin, *terra*) world. "...[T]he expanse [or firmament of heaven]" is a way to intensify what he is saying–not the heavens in some non-distinct way, but the heavens, the entirety of the celestial realm that is visible to the eye and beyond. David is not just talking about what the human eye can see, even using a high-powered scope. He is talking about the expanse which is inclusive of all of God's creative work or the entire created realm. Genesis 1 sheds light on what David is saying (Gen. 1:1-8, 14-19).

[1] In the beginning God created the heavens and the earth. [2] The earth was formless and void, and darkness was over the surface of the deep, and the Spirit of God was moving over the surface of the waters. [3] Then God said, "Let there be light"; and there was light. [4] God saw that the light was good; and God separated the light from the darkness. [5] God called the light day, and the darkness He called night. And there was evening and there was morning, one day. [6] Then God said, "Let there be an expanse in the midst of the waters, and let it separate the waters from the waters." [7] God made the expanse, and separated the waters which were below the expanse from the waters which were above the expanse; and it was so. [8] God called the expanse heaven. And there was evening and there was morning, a second day. (Gen. 1:1-8)

[14] Then God said, "Let there be lights in the expanse of the heavens to separate the day from the night, and let them be for signs and for seasons and for days and years; [15] and let them be for lights in the expanse of the heavens to give light on the earth"; and it was so. [16] God made the two great lights, the greater light to

govern the day, and the lesser light to govern the night; *He made* the stars also. [17] God placed them in the expanse of the heavens to give light on the earth, [18] and to govern the day and the night, and to separate the light from the darkness; and God saw that it was good. [19] There was evening and there was morning, a fourth day. (Gen. 1:14-19)

David is speaking about the sky, the wind, the stars, the moon, the sun and how those were put there by God to distinguish between days and nights and to create different signs and seasons and years and to provide energy to sustain life on the earth in order that God's glory, His majestic power, would be displayed for all to see.

God's natural book is truly amazing. There may be as many as 400 billion (give or take 200 billion) stars in each of the possible billions of galaxies that exist. The sun is one star in the vast array of our galaxy, the Milky Way. At night, the best we can do with our eyes is to see approximately 2,500 stars at once. But the Milky Way is not the only galaxy in God's heavens. There may be as many as 100 billion galaxies with 400 billion stars in each. As far as we know, the closest star to our solar system is about 30 trillion miles from us. Traveling at 30,000 miles per hour, it would take over 100,000 years to get there. If we could travel at 30 million miles per hour it would take more than 100 years. And yet all of that sits up there, sustained without the aid of man or machines or computers. The heavens declare the glory of God.

David also tells us how God's natural book functions in relation to man. What do the heavens and their expanse do in relation to man? How do they function? Do they just sit there quietly open for anyone to interpret them any way they want? Or do they speak to us. Psalm 19:1a says, "The heavens are telling [or "declaring"] the glory of God…" To tell or declare here means to make clear, to free from obscurity, to make known to the understating, to exhibit or show to the eye. What is being told or declared by the heavens? What is being made clear by the heavens? What is being freed from obscurity? The answer is the glory of God, the amazingness of God, the grandeur of God, the outshining of the dazzling brilliance of God, the fact that God is powerful, wise, awesome, and is worthy of our worship. The heavens declare His very existence. Romans 1:19-21 says:

> [19] because that which is known about God is evident within them; for God made it evident to them. [20] For since the creation of the world His invisible attributes, His eternal power and divine nature, have been clearly seen, being understood through what has been made, so that they are without excuse. [21] For even though they knew God, they did not honor Him as God or give thanks, but they became futile in their speculations, and their foolish heart was darkened. (Rom. 1:19-21)

Hebrews 3:4 says, "....every house is built by someone, but He who built all things is God."

Billboards cover the valley in which I live. Many of these contain advertisements for new homes. The billboards reveal who is building the home. The name of the builder carries value with it due to a reputation built up over many years. But how much more so with God who has made all things by the word of His power?

The expanse of heaven declares or shows "the work of His hands..." The heavens show the skillful work of God's hands, that is, His power. He created this giant machine we call the universe. In all its vastness, in all its complexity, in all of its mind-stretching, mind-boggling intricacy, and in all its precise orderliness, we have God's work displayed before our very eyes every day and every night and in every place. He is the master-craftsman behind all that we see and all that we do not see. The universe is like a theater which constantly shows the same movie, over and over and over, again and again and again. The glory of God is now and forever playing for all to see.

When we get caught up in the amazing glory of God displayed in creation, comparing ourselves as an ant hill to Mount Everest just does not fit. The contrast is not great enough, but it does help us get it into our minds. That is why Psalm 57:5 says, "Be exalted, O God, above the heavens; *Let* Your glory *be* above all the earth." In one sense, He is exalted above the heavens and His glory is above the earth. What the Psalmist desires is the conscious awareness and explicit recognition of the exaltation of God in the souls of men. Is this true of your soul?

The focused elaboration concerning God's natural book

Psalm 19:2-3 says, "Day to day pours forth speech, And night to night reveals knowledge. There is no speech, nor are there words; Their voice is not heard." Every day and night, the heavens declare the glory of God, and it is there for all to see. No one can escape it. The day and night are speaking to us, though not with words we can hear. Everyone hears them without audible words.

In Psalm 19:4-6, the sun is marked out as a singular display of God's glory revealed to all the world every day.

> [4] Their line has gone out through all the earth, And their utterances to the end of the world. In them He has placed a tent for the sun, [5] Which is as a bridegroom coming out of his chamber; It rejoices as a strong man to run his course. [6] Its rising is from one end of the heavens, And its circuit to the other end of them; And there is nothing hidden from its heat. (Psa. 19:4-6)

The sun is God's circuit preacher (v. 6). The sun burns at about 6,000 degrees centigrade on its surface. It travels in its orbit at 155 miles per second, which means it will take about 200 million years to complete one orbit around our galaxy. In all of this we see intelligent design, specific purpose, amazing beauty, unimaginable power, blazing majesty, but we do not yet see all of God's glory.

> [7] "He stretches out the north over empty space And hangs the earth on nothing. [8] "He wraps up the waters in His clouds, And the cloud does not burst under them. [9] "He obscures the face of the full moon And spreads His cloud over it. [10] "He has inscribed a circle on the surface of the waters At the boundary of light and darkness. [11] "The pillars of heaven tremble And are amazed at His rebuke. [12] "He quieted the sea with His power, And by His understanding He shattered Rahab. [13] "By His breath the heavens are cleared; His hand has pierced the fleeing serpent. [14] "Behold, these are the fringes of His ways; And how faint a word we hear of

Him! But His mighty thunder, who can understand?" (Job 26:7-
14)

As much as the glory of God is clearly seen in that which He has
created, it is only "the fringes of His ways" (Job 26:14).

Implications of Psalm 19:1-6

*We see in the heavens the awesomeness of God displayed every day
and in every place.*

The song "Our God is an awesome God" is right. At the end of
Genesis 1:15, we read, "and it was so." What was so? The beginning
of the verse reads, "and let them be for lights in the expanse of the
heavens to give light on the earth..." What Moses describes in a
somewhat casual manner is, in actuality, an amazing display of
divine power resulting in the manifestation of the glory of God.
Genesis 1:16b says, "He made the stars also." This post-script is
another indication of the power and glory of God in creation. Isaiah
40:25-28 says:

> [25] "To whom then will you liken Me That I would be *his* equal?"
> says the Holy One. [26] Lift up your eyes on high And see who has
> created these *stars*, The One who leads forth their host by number,
> He calls them all by name; Because of the greatness of His might
> and the strength of *His* power, Not one *of them* is missing. [27] Why
> do you say, O Jacob, and assert, O Israel, "My way is hidden from
> the LORD, And the justice due me escapes the notice of my God? [28]
> Do you not know? Have you not heard? The Everlasting God, the
> LORD, the Creator of the ends of the earth Does not become weary
> or tired. His understanding is inscrutable. (Isa. 40:25-28)

"The heavens are telling of the glory of God" (Psa. 19:1a), but not
all of it.

Why doesn't everyone acknowledge this?

The answer to this excellent question is because something is wrong with us. Listen to Romans 1:18-25.

> [18] For the wrath of God is revealed from heaven against all ungodliness and unrighteousness of men who suppress the truth in unrighteousness, [19] because that which is known about God is evident within them; for God made it evident to them. [20] For since the creation of the world His invisible attributes, His eternal power and divine nature, have been clearly seen, being understood through what has been made, so that they are without excuse. [21] For even though they knew God, they did not honor Him as God or give thanks, but they became futile in their speculations, and their foolish heart was darkened. [22] Professing to be wise, they became fools, [23] and exchanged the glory of the incorruptible God for an image in the form of corruptible man and of birds and four-footed animals and crawling creatures. [24] Therefore God gave them over in the lusts of their hearts to impurity, so that their bodies would be dishonored among them. [25] For they exchanged the truth of God for a lie, and worshiped and served the creature rather than the Creator, who is blessed forever. Amen. (Rom. 1:18-25)

Man's ability to receive and acknowledge the revelation of God's glory in creation is like trying to listen to an AM radio at night. It is all distorted. God's revelation in creation gets through, but is denied for what it is, though man knows better deep down in the dark crevices of his soul.

Something more than creation is needed for man to receive and acknowledge God's revelation in creation properly since the entrance of sin. Man's ability to see God's glory in creation and acknowledge it for what it is has been ruined. Creation displays Gods' power, which ought to produce worship and adoration in us, but it does not. We need a re-creation of soul. We need renovation. We need spiritual renewal. We need what only the Holy Spirit can give us–new eyes, new ears, new minds, new hearts, and new wills. There is good news. Jesus Christ came and as a reward for His life-unto-death obedience, He was given the Holy Spirit to be sent to enlighten the eyes of blind sinners to see the glory of God in the face of Christ.

We see in man a selective irrationality.

Most people in our day deny most if not all that I have said. But what is the alternative view? Some say the big-bang theory of origins. Really? What do explosions produce? Do they produce order or chaos? Others argue for evolution based on their view of the evidence. Yet this is done with no evidence of life-forms going through the transitional process of mutation. This process is assumed to answer the question of origins and is brought to the evidence, but it is not part of the evidence examined. By the way, cells cannot be reduced to something other than what they are without ceasing to function. In other words, they cannot mutate, morph, or change. All the various parts and pieces of a cell work together interdependently. When it comes to cells and their parts, it is all for one and one for all.

Many people are of the "I'll believe it when I see it" mentality. Yet no one was there to see the so-called first explosion. No one has ever seen an ape turning into a man, except in pictures or movies. And no one has ever seen a cell mutate, but evolution is scientifically proven? That does not sound very scientific. To deny anything and everything unless you see it does not work in the world in which we live. For example, we cannot see numerical values, but we all use them and no one denies they exist. We cannot see the laws of logic, but we all use them and no one denies they exist (except radical skeptics who use principles of logic to deny logic). We cannot see air, but we all use it and no one, in his right mind, denies it exists. Suppose someone wanted to deny that air exists. The person would be forced to use it while arguing against it. This is a real dilemma. We cannot see the soul, thoughts, feelings, and emotions, but we all know these things exist and must have some sort of explanation for their existence. What's the best explanation for these things? Everything that exists is ultimately caused to exist by God, who exists eternally, and who has made us rational creatures who, for example, utilize the laws of logic without scientific proof and though they cannot be proven by observation. They exist because God exists.

Why, then, does the unbelieving world often ridicule biblical creationism and the church for believing it? It may be because of what we project. Could it be that part of the problem is that we Christians often project a very dim light to the on-looking world? Albert Einstein apparently acknowledged an author for the universe, but was not a church-going man. One man comments on Einstein's acknowledgment and little use for organized religion as follows:

> The design of the universe…is very magnificent and shouldn't be taken for granted. In fact, I believe that is why Einstein had so little use for organized religion… He must have looked at what the preachers said about God and felt that they were blaspheming. My guess is that he simply felt that religions he'd run across did not have proper respect…for the author of the universe.[1]

Preachers need to insure that they are proclaiming God's Word in such a manner that hearers at least come away acknowledging that the preacher thinks God is due respect and awe from the souls of men. The same goes for the verbal witness of the everyday Christian.

Another reason why biblical creationism is ridiculed has nothing at all to do with the church and its preachers. Something is wrong with man. As noted above, man's ability to receive and properly acknowledge the revelation of God's glory in creation is not what it was in the beginning. The first man, Adam, sinned. He became morally polluted and that same pollution affects everyone. Though we know God is and that He is powerful, we suppress the truth in unrighteousness. Listen to the words of the Apostle Paul already quoted above.

---

[1] Quoted in John Piper, *Let the Nations be Glad: The Supremacy of God in Missions* (Grand Rapids: Baker Books, 1993, sixth printing 1996), 12.

[18] For the wrath of God is revealed from heaven against all ungodliness and unrighteousness of men who suppress the truth in unrighteousness, [19] because that which is known about God is evident within them; for God made it evident to them. [20] For since the creation of the world His invisible attributes, His eternal power and divine nature, have been clearly seen, being understood through what has been made, so that they are without excuse. (Rom. 1:18-20)

The problem is not that there is no evidence for God's existence. The problem is what we do with the evidence.

Man in sin is like the fellow who was convinced he was dead. His wife sent him to the doctor to verify that he was alive. After talking to him for quite some time and showing him that he was still breathing, he had a pulse, his heart was beating, and he could still talk and hear, the doctor asked him, "Do dead men bleed?" The man replied, "Well, of course not. Dead men don't bleed." The doctor grabbed a needle and poked the man's arm. He started to bleed, and then exclaimed, "Well, what do you know, dead men do bleed after all!" This man believed something that was against all the evidence. He conditioned his mind to believe that he was dead no matter what. Any proof brought to him was easily dismissed by using an irrational, scape-goat argument that the man brought with him to the discussion table. This is similar to what man in sin does. He believes that we are improved upon billion year-old pond soup, or we are a complex of random-chance chemical reactions, or we are products of a primal explosion, or we exist in a materialistic world where everything may be analyzed by one or more of our five senses.

Let us think some more about the "I'll believe it when I see it" mentality. This is based on what is called empiricism. This theory asserts that all knowledge is gained by observation. I once read of a story about an empiricist Russian cosmonaut. As the story goes, he radioed back to earth, "We are here in space and I can assure you that God does not exist because I do not see Him." A Christian theologian replied, "If you would open the space-ship door, you would see Him immediately." I am not sure if that is a true story but I do know it illustrates my point that some people are of the "I'll believe it when I see it" mind-set. But is that way of thinking, that philosophy of knowledge, reasonable?

All agree that we have five senses–taste, touch, smell, sight, and hearing. The empiricist says that everything we know is gained by observation. But what about the *claim* that everything we know is gained by observation? We cannot observe the theory or the claim that all we know is gained by observation. A theory is not a physical entity. A theory or claim may be tested, but it cannot be seen. How can the empiricist *know* that all knowledge is gained through observation? To know something means to have mental cognition of the thing known. You cannot see mental cognition. You cannot see the theory of empiricism; you may only assume it, but once you do, you have denied it applies to justify itself. So either you must acknowledge that you have unproven presuppositions or you must be satisfied with irrationalism and contradiction.

We may do the same thing with the materialist. A materialist believes that all things that exist are made up of matter–something that takes up space, something that is concrete, objective, and able to be touched. However, materialism is a theory, which is not comprised of matter. Theories are not physical entities; they do not extend in space. As a matter of fact, materialists utilize the laws of logic to observe the world and make non-contradictory statements about the world. Neither the laws of logic nor propositions are material. So the materialist actually contradicts his own theory by trying to argue for it using immaterial laws of logic.

The Christian theory of knowledge, otherwise known as epistemology, is that since God made man in His image (Gen. 1:26), in some senses man reflects God, though very poorly due to our sin. Man reflects God in the fact and manner in which he knows, thinks, and communicates. Neither empiricism nor materialism can account for itself and both actually borrow something from the biblical worldview–the laws of logic and the existence of non-material entities. This is knowledge-theory or epistemological theft. The denial of God actually assumes things like the laws of logic or non-material entities which may only be justified or accounted for in a Christian worldview.

This futile way of thinking is exactly why we need Jesus Christ. The glory of the gospel is Jesus Christ, the great physician of souls. He heals our souls. He fixes them. He transforms them. He makes them able to acknowledge and proclaim God's glory in creation and redemption.

Chapter 5

The Revelatory Function of Creation (II):
Creation testifies of His existence

Creation testifies of God's existence. We saw this from Psalm 19 in the last chapter. This chapter will attempt to show the same from Romans 1:20, which says, "For since the creation of the world His invisible attributes, His eternal power and divine nature, have been clearly seen, being understood through what has been made, so that they are without excuse" (Rom. 1:20). This chapter will also illustrate the theology of Romans 1:20 from the Apostle Paul's ministry recorded in Acts 14. We will see that Paul took his theology with him when he confronted idolatry in a place called Lystra.

Romans 1:20 in Context

Paul's epistle to the Romans is an exposition of the gospel. "For I am not ashamed of the gospel, for it is the power of God for salvation to everyone who believes, to the Jew first and also to the Greek" (Rom. 1:16). This is very important to remember. In Romans 1:18-3:20 Paul deals with the universal guilt of mankind. All of us have the same problem. We are guilty before God because we are sinners. This is the universal plight of man–sin, lawlessness, breaking the law of God, which leads to guilt and condemnation. In Romans 3:21ff. Paul announces God's solution to man's problem–the gospel, the good news of Christ for us, God providing righteousness for sinners all by grace through faith alone. Romans 1:18ff. comes in this context of the bad news that is true of all of us. We are sinners. We are guilty and we have no legitimate excuse that gets us off of God's hook of judgment.

Paul's purpose in the first section of this book is to show the universal sin and guilt of man. He is speaking theologically, writing to believers in Christ. He is making assertions which remind the believers of the universal problem of human sin. Here Paul is writing as a Christian theologian to Christian people painting the horrible background to the wonderful news of the gospel. Man is ungodly. Man is unrighteous. Man is not good. Man is in trouble with God because of what he does with the knowledge of God that he possesses.

Explanation of Romans 1:20

Paul says, "For since the creation of the world His invisible attributes, His eternal power and divine nature, have been clearly seen, being understood through what has been made, so that they are without excuse" (Rom. 1:20). Here Paul tells us that certain things are testified to by that which has been made. I use the word "testify" here to refer to non-verbal revelation by and about God. God is both the subject and object of this revelation. In Romans 1:20, Paul asserts that some things are known about God, "being understood through what has been made." The creation, that which has been made by God, testifies of, witnesses to, or confesses its maker, though without words. One other point is important before we continue. Notice what Romans 1:19 does not say.

> [18] For the wrath of God is revealed from heaven against all ungodliness and unrighteousness of men who suppress the truth in unrighteousness, [19] because that which is known about God is evident within them; for God made it evident to them. (Rom. 1:18-19)

It does not say "that which *can be* known about God is evident within them..." When Paul speaks of creation's testifying and witnessing function, he speaks of an effective function. In other words, creation's theological message gets through to everyone. The problem is not that creation's message does not get through. The problem is what we do with it. As we will see later, although creation's theological message gets through to everyone, it helps no one get out of trouble with God. What things does the created realm teach us about God?

God has invisible attributes.

"For since the creation of the world His invisible attributes, His eternal power and divine nature, have been clearly seen, being understood through what has been made, so that they are without excuse" (Rom. 1:20). What does Paul mean by "attributes"? These are sometimes called God's properties or perfections. An attribute is a term we use to describe, in this case, an aspect of God. But we need to be careful here. An attribute is not a part of God, like a piece of a pie is a part of a whole pie. God does not have parts. There is no part of God that is *this* and another part of God that is *that*. All of God is all that God is. Also, in studying the attributes of God we are not exhausting the meaning of who and what God is. Again, attributes seek to describe an aspect of God revealed to us, not the totality of who God is. Only God knows Himself like that. We may only know God in so far as He has revealed Himself and no creature knows, or even can know, God as God knows Himself. God is infinite. We are finite.

Notice that these are called "*invisible* attributes." They cannot be seen, in themselves, but they may be, as Paul says, "clearly seen, [that is] understood through what has been made..." So Paul is saying that certain invisible attributes of God are clearly seen, even understood by men and women by the effect produced (that is, by creation, or by that which has been made by God, which is everything other than God). This is like saying, "Every house has a builder and the builder of all things is God." That which is built reflects something of the one who built it.

We need to be careful here. Paul is not saying that *everything* there is to know about God is known by that which has been made. He is not saying that if man studies creation he may know God perfectly, exhaustively, and even as God knows Himself. As a matter of fact, as mentioned above, since God is eternal, we cannot

and will never know all there is to know about Him. The finite
(man) cannot contain the infinite (God). So Paul is not claiming that
all that God is is revealed through that which has been made. As Job
said, God's works of creation and providence are only "the fringes
of His ways" (Job 26:14). Paul is saying that everyone knows
something about God but (as we will see) this knowledge helps no
one get out of trouble with Him. What are His invisible attributes
clearly seen, being understood by that which has been made?

God possesses eternal power.

God's eternal power is clearly seen, being understood through what
has been made. Power refers to divine energy, might, the ability to
act. In God's case, this means He can do whatsoever pleases Him.
Psalm 135:6, "Whatever the LORD pleases, He does, In heaven and in
earth, in the seas and in all deeps." This is unlike us. Our power is
limited and temporal. God's power is unlimited and eternal. God
does whatever He pleases, whenever and wherever He wants to. We
get exhausted. The LORD our God never tires or gets weary. We can
desire to do more than we have the ability to do. This is not so with
God. "Whatever the Lord pleases, He does."

The adjective "eternal" refers to that which has always existed,
that which is not bounded or hedged in by time or any other created
entity. The things that have been made had a beginning. They are
not eternal. There was a time when everything, other than God, was
not. He who brought all things into existence was not Himself
brought into existence. God is outside of that which comes into
existence. All things which come into existence are outside of Him.
Everything outside of God is not God. All things which come into
existence are external to Him who called them into existence
because He is eternal and they are temporal. We are not eternal. We
are hedged in by time. Our strength is limited. We get tired. We get
exhausted. Eternal power knows no exhausting. God exerts power
without depletion.

Paul's point is that a temporal creation (and its continued
existence) argues the invisible, eternal power of God for its

existence. At some point in going back from your own existence, there must be a cause unlike that which is caused.

Many years ago, I read a book where the author was discussing a statement made by a Harvard geneticist and Marxist named Richard Lewontin. Lewontin was arguing for materialism as opposed to theism. Here is what he said:

> It is not that the methods and institutions of science somehow compel us to accept a material explanation of the phenomenal world [that is, science does not explain or prove the origin of matter], on the contrary, that we are forced by our a priori adherence to material causes to create an apparatus of investigation and a set of concepts that produce material explanations, no matter how counter-intuitive, no matter how mystifying to the uninitiated. Moreover, that materialism is absolute, for we cannot allow a divine Foot in the door. ...To appeal to an omnipotent deity is to allow that at any moment the regularities of nature may be ruptured, that miracles may happen.[1]

I could not have said it better myself. A theory is already in place before the facts of the material world are considered on their own. When those who adhere to this type of materialism get to define the terms for debate, it is a waste of time to argue about the evidence. As a matter of fact, we should not argue about evidences. We should simply proclaim them, but within a biblical worldview. The penetrating Christian apologist will attempt to get behind the facts and arguments to the philosophy of fact which their opponent brings to the facts. According to Paul, the material universe argues the God of eternal power who never came into existence, made all things and sustains all things. And that eternal power is possessed by the God who reveals Himself in creation and the Bible. Anything that causes all material things to come into existence must first exist non-materially. Things that first come into existence do not produce themselves. These things are evident to all men, though suppressed in unrighteousness.

---

[1] Quoted in Phillip E. Johnson, *Defeating Darwinism by Opening Minds* (Downers Grove, IL: InterVarsity Press, 1997), 81.

God's nature is divine.

The word "nature" refers to that which makes up the primary qualities of an object or person. It is often used as a functional equivalent of "essence." In this case, Paul is saying that the God he is referring to is divine, true deity, the one and only true God. He alone possesses that which makes up divinity, and His divinity is clearly seen, being understood through what has been made. That which is above the creation becomes known by creatures due to the act and implications of creation. In other words, man knows God inescapably by that which He has made; and he knows that God is not like that which has been made. That which has been made implies the maker that is and none other; and the maker of all things is the God of the Bible.

Practical Observations from Romans 1:20

This knowledge of God is universally possessed and universally suppressed.

Romans 1:18-20 is worth reading again:

> [18] For the wrath of God is revealed from heaven against all ungodliness and unrighteousness of men who suppress the truth in unrighteousness, [19] because that which is known about God is evident within them; for God made it evident to them. [20] For since the creation of the world His invisible attributes, His eternal power and divine nature, have been clearly seen, being understood through what has been made, so that they are without excuse. (Rom. 1:18-20)

This universally possessed and universally suppressed knowledge of God is where the non-Christian religions of the world come from. All men have an innate knowledge that God is and due to our messed up souls, we invent practices we think will sooth the divine.

This knowledge of God has ethical implications.

There are universal *oughts* which derive from this knowledge. According to Romans 1:21, "honor" and "thanks" are due to God by virtue of creation. "For even though they knew God, they did not honor Him as God or give thanks, but they became futile in their speculations, and their foolish heart was darkened" (Rom. 1:21). Though many give a nod to God here and there, no one gives honor and thanks to Him perfectly and perpetually, though He is certainly worthy of such. Something is wrong with us.

This knowledge of God does not stop us from sinning, even though we know that sin brings consequences.

Here is Romans 1:28-32.

> [28] And just as they did not see fit to acknowledge God any longer, God gave them over to a depraved mind, to do those things which are not proper, [29] being filled with all unrighteousness, wickedness, greed, evil; full of envy, murder, strife, deceit, malice; *they are* gossips, [30] slanderers, haters of God, insolent, arrogant, boastful, inventors of evil, disobedient to parents, [31] without understanding, untrustworthy, unloving, unmerciful; [32] and although they know the ordinance of God, that those who practice such things are worthy of death, they not only do the same, but also give hearty approval to those who practice them. (Rom. 1:28-32)

We know we will be held accountable, but that does not stop us. We know that the justice of God will catch up to us, but the best that knowledge does is to keep us from being worse than we are. At its worst, the knowledge of a coming day of reckoning produces in us "hearty approval to those who practice" sin, which puts a band-aid over our own guilty souls. We approve the sins of others to justify our own. It is like the old argument, "Everyone is doing it, so it must be right." But human might does not make right in God's court of equity.

This knowledge of God that all men possess via creation helps no one get out of trouble with God.

Something is way, way wrong. Because He made all things, He is worthy of glory, and honor, and thanks, and praise. But He is given just the opposite. The limited knowledge of God all men possess is not enough. It is real knowledge. It is knowledge that is actually possessed. Everyone has it, but it does not get us out of trouble with God. In fact, it gets us in more trouble because that which we possess we suppress. We need help. We need remedial knowledge.

This knowledge of God, though not remedial, is the background because of which the remedial knowledge of the gospel comes.

Romans 3:21ff. is God's remedy, God's gift.

> [21] But now apart from the Law *the* righteousness of God has been manifested, being witnessed by the Law and the Prophets, [22] even *the* righteousness of God through faith in Jesus Christ for all those who believe; for there is no distinction; [23] for all have sinned and fall short of the glory of God, [24] being justified as a gift by His grace through the redemption which is in Christ Jesus; (Rom. 3:21-24)

The gospel, the good news about what Christ has done, is God's method of saving us, not helping us to save ourselves or helping God to save us. We need the remedial knowledge of God. We need the saving knowledge of God and this must come from God Himself and it does, in the Bible alone. The incarnation of the Son of God is God on mission to save the lost. The Son as Savior is revealed in the Bible alone. The Bible is because sin is and God has a plan of redemption. Do not settle for acknowledging that God is creator and preserver. Acknowledge that you are a sinner with needs that you, nor anyone else, can meet. Christ, and Christ alone, however, can!

Acts 14:17–God's Patience and Goodness in the Teeth of Idolatry

The book of Romans is a theological work by the Apostle Paul. In this section, I want to turn briefly from the writing theologian to examine the same theologian as a preacher and witness of the gospel. Paul's travels as a preacher are recounted for us in the book of Acts. Here is Acts 14:8-18.

> [8] At Lystra a man was sitting who had no strength in his feet, lame from his mother's womb, who had never walked. [9] This man was listening to Paul as he spoke, who, when he had fixed his gaze on him and had seen that he had faith to be made well, [10] said with a loud voice, "Stand upright on your feet." And he leaped up and *began* to walk. [11] When the crowds saw what Paul had done, they raised their voice, saying in the Lycaonian language, "The gods have become like men and have come down to us." [12] And they *began* calling Barnabas, Zeus, and Paul, Hermes, because he was the chief speaker. [13] The priest of Zeus, whose *temple* was just outside the city, brought oxen and garlands to the gates, and wanted to offer sacrifice with the crowds. [14] But when the apostles Barnabas and Paul heard of it, they tore their robes and rushed out into the crowd, crying out [15] and saying, "Men, why are you doing these things? We are also men of the same nature as you, and preach the gospel to you that you should turn from these vain things to a living God, WHO MADE THE HEAVEN AND THE EARTH AND THE SEA AND ALL THAT IS IN THEM. [16] "In the generations gone by He permitted all the nations to go their own ways; [17] and yet He did not leave Himself without witness, in that He did good and gave you rains from heaven and fruitful seasons, satisfying your hearts with food and gladness." [18] *Even* saying these things, with difficulty they restrained the crowds from offering sacrifice to them. (Acts 14:8-18)

Context of and Brief Observations from Acts 14:8-18

This is part of Paul's first missionary journey. Paul and Barnabas were sent from the church in Antioch, Syria. They traveled north and west from Antioch to various places and then back to their home church. They had to flee Iconium due to some Jews who did not believe and who were stirring up others against them (Acts 14:1-7). They were going about preaching the gospel (Acts 14:7, 15). Luke's account is probably an overview and not a detailed word-for-word rehearsal of all that was said and done. It is also of interest to note that Paul and Barnabas are confronting idolatry (Acts 14:15). In the midst of this idolatry, Paul says, "and yet He did not leave Himself without witness, in that He did good and gave you rains from heaven and fruitful seasons, satisfying your hearts with food and gladness" (Acts 14:17). Let us think through some practical implications of this account.

Some Practical Implications

The idolatry of ancient religion called for repentance.

> ...Men, why are you doing these things? We are also men of the same nature as you, and preach the gospel to you that you should turn from these vain things to a living God, WHO MADE THE HEAVEN AND THE EARTH AND THE SEA AND ALL THAT IS IN THEM. (Act 14:15)

Paul and Barnabas do not argue against religion in itself; they argue against false religion. These folks had misplaced religious inclinations in their souls. They had the notion that deity existed, but they had distorted the truth, just as Paul wrote about in Romans 1. Paul and Barnabas confronted false religion with true religion. They confronted idolatry with the gospel of Jesus Christ. The gospel is remedial knowledge. Paul's remedy to idolatry, his solution for man's problem, is not to believe that God is and that He is powerful and that He is good and that He is kind, and that He is patient. It is the gospel!

The providence of God toward the nations is a display of God's patience.

"In the generations gone by He permitted all the nations to go their own ways" (Acts 14:16). Douglas Kelly says, "God had mercifully overlooked their sins of idolatry without passing destructive judgment upon them."[2] Paul says elsewhere:

> [3] But do you suppose this, O man, when you pass judgment on those who practice such things and do the same *yourself*, that you will escape the judgment of God? [4] Or do you think lightly of the riches of His kindness and tolerance and patience, not knowing that the kindness of God leads you to repentance? [5] But because of your stubbornness and unrepentant heart you are storing up wrath for yourself in the day of wrath and revelation of the righteous judgment of God, (Rom. 2:3-5)

Consider God's patience. Every day, all over the world, idolatry takes place. The religions of the world are a perversion of the natural knowledge of God. This perversion of what we know about God is sinful, yet God permits us to live. Why is this? He has purposes of grace He is working out. God's purpose of grace toward us in Christ has a spill-over effect on account of which His patience is displayed. Why hasn't the judgment taken place yet? God's patience is working in conjunction with His grace to move more to repentance (2 Pet. 3:9). We may know of God's patience by His continued acts of tending to His creation and not bringing swift and universal judgment, but in order to be right with God, we need the gospel. The good news of the gospel is remedial news. It is the one and only remedy for our problem.

The providence of God toward the nations also displays the goodness of God toward His creation.

[16] In the generations gone by He permitted all the nations to go

---

[2] Kelly, *Systematic Theology*, I:139.

their own ways; [17] and yet He did not leave Himself without witness, in that He did good and gave you rains from heaven and fruitful seasons, satisfying your hearts with food and gladness. (Acts 14:16-17)

God supplies our physical needs. He brings satisfaction to our hearts with food and gladness. He gives us what we do not deserve. This is mercy to those who do not deserve it. Think upon God's goodness. He gives food. He causes it to rain. He insures that season after season comes one after another, along with fruitfulness. Yet all of this is done to a world of idolaters. We may know of God's goodness by His continued acts of tending to His creation, but in order to be right with God, we need the gospel.

The knowledge of God we possess via creation and providence is not sufficient to secure the well-being of our souls.

Listen to the Confession of Faith again:

Although the light of nature, and the works of creation and providence do so far manifest the goodness, wisdom and power of God, as to leave men unexcusable; yet are they not sufficient to give that knowledge of God and His will, which is necessary unto Salvation. (BCF 1689, 1.1)

This is why the Bible exists. The Bible does not merely duplicate what may be known of God intuitively by creation and providence. The Bible is the revelation of knowledge not possessed by virtue of being created in God's image (Gen. 1:26) or by virtue of studying the natural order (Psa. 19:1-6). The knowledge of God revealed in Scripture is unique. It is revelation with a distinct purpose. It is knowledge calculated to repair the problems brought on mankind by the entrance of sin into the world. It is remedial knowledge. In other words, Scripture is necessary due to the limitations of General Revelation and God's purpose to rescue man from the consequences of sin. Holy Scripture is because sin is and redemption is. Sin has made redemptive or salvific revelation necessary. The Bible is

God's deposit of that knowledge necessary for the salvation of souls. This means that the gospel cannot be (and never could be) learned from the stars. The Trinity is a doctrine revealed in the Bible not through eggs (i.e., shell, egg-white, and yoke). Every analogy from nature always breaks down and ends up trivializing the sacred. The only place to find the saving, infallible knowledge of the true God and the one way of salvation is in the Bible alone. The only sufficient knowledge of God to secure the well-being of our souls is found in Holy Scripture.

We are reminded of the love, mercy, and compassion of God.

Listen to John Owen:

> It was, indeed, out of infinite love, mercy, and compassion, that God would at all reveal his mind and will unto sinners. He might for ever have locked up the treasures of his wisdom and prudence, wherein he abounds towards us in his Word, in his own eternal breast. He might have left all the sons of men unto that woeful darkness, whereinto by sin they had cast themselves, and kept them, with the angels who sinned before them, under the chains and power of it, unto the judgment of the great day. But from infinite love he condescended to reveal himself and his will unto us.[3]

The Bible is God's testimony of His condescending love to sinners, centering upon Jesus Christ, the incarnate Son of God. It was for us and for our salvation that the Son of God assumed human nature. And it was for us and for our salvation that God took the time to record His way of salvation in a book. Though creation testifies of God's existence, only Scripture reveals the way of salvation through Jesus Christ.

---

[3] Quoted in Shaw, *Westminster Confession*, 40.

Chapter 6

The Initial Act of Creation:
Creation out of nothing

I remember being in a university biology class and having to study about Charles Darwin's theory of origins–how life began. Since the professor and the textbook we used advocated Darwin's theory, I assumed it was proven by the facts and, when test time came, answered the questions to the best of my ability as the professor expected. This is a common experience. Since your grade depends on agreeing with the "experts," you had better agree.

A little over 15 years ago, a U.S. poll on evolution v. creation, reflective of the mid-60s to the mid-90s, said that 9% of U.S. citizens believed in the theory of naturalistic evolution and 91% held to some form of theism. About 45% held to biblical creationism and 45% held to theistic evolution. These numbers may shock you, as they did me when I first read them. Even Carl Sagan, however, a major proponent of naturalistic evolution, admitted this.

These numbers are shocking because it is not what appears to be due to the fact that the scientists (and those who hang on their every word) have the microphones, cameras, public school classrooms, and government and private funding on their side. For instance, a NOVA video, *The Miracle of Life*, used by some public school districts at least in the past opens with these lines:

Four and a half billion years ago, the young planet Earth was a mass of cosmic dust and particles. It was almost completely engulfed by the shallow primordial seas. Powerful winds gathered random molecules from the atmosphere. Some were deposited in the seas. Tides and currents swept the molecules together. And somewhere in this ancient ocean the miracle of life began.

...From these one-celled organisms evolved all life on earth. And the foundation of life, the cell, has endured unchanged since the first tiny organisms swam in the cradle of life, the sea.[1]

When that philosophy is published in an expensive text book, read by millions of students, taught by thousands of teachers, and published as the way things were and are in magazines over a period of time it is assumed to be the truth.

But how do they know that? Were they there to run tests, to establish hypotheses, to test them, confirm their findings, and draw universally assured conclusions? Obviously not. How do the experts draw such conclusions? Where did the winds come from, the seas, and the molecules? And how come everything evolves over billions of years and adapts to new conditions brought on by the evolutionary process except the cell, the foundation of life or what they call the miracle of life? Do they believe in miracles? These are questions worth asking and scientists are still trying to find their answers.

One of the most well-known and debated texts in the Bible is, unfortunately, its first verse. "In the beginning God created the heavens and the earth" (Gen. 1:1). What appears to be a very simple and straight-forward assertion often gets lost in a maze of bewilderment and doubt. Its simplicity does not in any way reduce its profundity. In fact, its simplicity and straight-forwardness are probably why some seek to either deny its teaching or tweak it so much that if Moses, the author of this text, could roll over in his grave, he would. Packed into these ten words in our English translation is more than meets the eye and has been the cause of both unspeakable wonder and amazement and utter denial and even disgust. What I want to do with this text is explain it, allow the Bible to draw out some implications from it, and interact a little with those who differ.

---

[1] Johnson, *Defeating Darwinism*, 123.

Explanation of Genesis 1:1

Its Broad Biblical Context

We must remember that the author of Genesis, Moses, was not present at the events he recounts for us in the book of Genesis. He is recounting something that no man was there to see. He was not standing by writing fast and furious as each day of creation occurred. Either God revealed the creation account directly to Moses or it was passed down to him.

It is also important to realize who Moses is writing to and for what purpose. He is not writing to a board of scientists. He is not writing to a twenty-first-century audience. From all we know, Moses wrote Genesis after ancient Israel was brought out of Egypt by the mighty hand of God and prior to entering into the land of Canaan. So he is writing to remind the ancient people of God where they came from and how their history related to the rest of the world. God's redemptive purposes on the earth are connected to the creation of all things.

The Structure of Genesis 1 and 2

Genesis 1:1 is a general and all-inclusive summary statement on creation. Genesis 1:2-31 gives a more detailed account of how God created all things ("the heavens and the earth"), in the space of six days. Genesis 2:1-3 summarizes God's all-inclusive creative activity and functions as the capstone of creation when the Creator enters His rest. Notice the first word of 2:1, "Thus."

> [1] Thus the heavens and the earth were completed, and all their hosts. [2] By the seventh day God completed His work which He had done, and He rested on the seventh day from all His work which He had done. [3] Then God blessed the seventh day and sanctified it, because in it He rested from all His work which God had created and made. (Gen. 2:1-3)

Genesis 2:4 functions as a sign-post indicating that the next section is going to narrow down its scope and concentrate on the pinnacle of creation–man in God's image.[2] It is of interest to note that the account of creation shines a spot-light on man in God's image (Gen. 1:26 and 2:4ff.), male and female, and from there Moses recounts the first sin and the effects it brought upon mankind and the earth itself (Gen. 3). This spot-light on man and his fall should tell us that man is important and sin is a big problem.

Exposition of Genesis 1:1

"In the beginning God created the heavens and the earth" (Gen. 1:1). Let us look at this verse in some detail. Notice the opening phrase, "In the beginning..." This refers to a point of time in the past. No long period of time is hinted at, witnessed also by the facts of the following details of a six day period used by God to create (more on this below). Moses is speaking about the beginning of all things created, all things that have come into being, all things that are not eternal. This speaks of "a particular point in eternity" where everything was brought "into existence out of nothing."[3]

Moses then identifies the subject or active agent of creation–"God." "In the beginning God..." At this point in eternity, God already was. God is from everlasting to everlasting. He did not come into being. God is; everything else becomes. Of all the names for God used in Scripture, one name best suits this verse and it is the name *Elohim.* And that is the word Moses used. It means the strong and mighty One. This word occurs here as no accident. What we are reading about is a display, an awesome display, of the power of a uniquely mighty Being. This One is unrivaled in might, unrivaled in strength, and unrivaled in power.

Then Moses adds the verb "created." This word is used only of God in Scripture. There are many words used for God making things. For instance, God "formed" Adam from what He had already

---

[2] Cf. Kelly, *Creation and Change,* 40-41 for a fuller discussion of the structure of Genesis 1-2.

[3] Kelly, *Creation and Change,* 51.

created (Gen. 2:7). But the word "created" refers to what God made out of nothing. This is creation *ex nihilo*–creation out of nothing. With no pre-existing materials, God created all things that exist; that is, everything outside of Himself. Matter, energy, natural laws–none of these are eternal. All things came into being, except God Himself, in the beginning.

Here we see a definite, intelligent, designed, controlled act of God. And we should expect that what God makes reflects a definiteness, intelligence, design, and control. God is not viewed as a cosmic mechanic here, working with pre-existing parts and putting them together. He is the cause of the material which comes into existence by His power.

What did God create in the beginning? The text tells us that He created "the heavens and the earth." This is a broad statement inclusive of everything made. Kelly comments:

> Heavens and earth is a way of saying 'everything that exists', whether galaxies, nebulae or solar systems; all things from the farthest reaches of outer space to the smallest grain of sand or bacterial microbe on planet earth; absolutely everything was created by God. ...'All things' include the various ranks of angels, and every form of life from whales and elephants to [non-pathogenic] viruses. ...every form of energy and matter; the speed of light, nuclear structure, electromagnetism and gravity, and all the laws by which nature operates.[4]

Psalm 33:6 and 9 say, "By the word of the LORD the heavens were made, And all the host of them by the breath of His mouth" and "[f]or He spoke, and it was done; He commanded, and it stood fast." Hebrews 3:4 says, "For every house is built by someone, but He who built all things is God." God and nature are distinct. Matter had a beginning. All things that came into existence were brought into existence without pre-existing materials. The English Puritan Thomas Watson offers these humbling words:

---

[4] Kelly, *Creation and Change*, 45.

God made the world without any pre-existent matter. This is the difference between generation and creation. In generation there is suitable material at hand, some matter to work upon; but in creation there is no pre-existent matter. God brought all this glorious fabric of the world out of the womb of nothing. Our beginning was of nothing. Some brag of their birth and ancestry; but how little cause have they to boast who came from nothing.[5]

The Bible and Genesis 1:1

The Bible clearly asserts here in Genesis 1:1, and in many other places, that the God of the Holy Scripture is the maker of heaven and earth. Hebrews 11:3 says, "By faith we understand that the worlds were framed by the word of God, so that the things which are seen were not made of things which are visible." That which has been made was not made by that which has been made. The maker of the things which are seen was not made by that which has been made. Again, only God is eternal–Father, Son and Holy Spirit. Everything else was made by Him.

The Bible also asserts that the God who created heaven and earth in the beginning is also the providential ruler over that which He made. In other words, there is a sovereign, divine care-taker over all things made. Listen to Psalm 135:5-12.

> [5] For I know that the LORD is great And that our Lord is above all gods. [6] Whatever the LORD pleases, He does, In heaven and in earth, in the seas and in all deeps. [7] He causes the vapors to ascend from the ends of the earth; Who makes lightnings for the rain, Who brings forth the wind from His treasuries. [8] He smote the firstborn of Egypt, Both of man and beast. [9] He sent signs and wonders into your midst, O Egypt, Upon Pharaoh and all his servants. [10] He smote many nations And slew mighty kings, [11] Sihon, king of the Amorites, And Og, king of Bashan, And all the

---

[5] Thomas Watson, *A Body of Divinity: Contained in Sermons upon the Westminster Assembly's Catechism* (Edinburgh and Carlisle, PA: The Banner of Truth Trust, 2000), 116.

kingdoms of Canaan; [12] And He gave their land as a heritage, A heritage to Israel His people. (Psa. 135:5-12)

We do not live in a closed system of reality, as already noted. We are not off-limits to the supernatural power and preservative care of God. Divine providence is

> the continuing act of divine power, subsequent to the act of creation, by means of which God preserves all things in being, supports their actions, governs them according to his established order, and directs them toward their ordained ends.[6]

The extent of divine providence encompasses all creatures and things. This includes animate and inanimate things–men and animals, trees and mountains, storms, earthquakes, kings, governments, freeway traffic, traffic accidents, doctor's visits, surgeries, marriages, aches, pains, jobs, and salaries. This is a great comfort for the believing soul.

Why does Genesis 1:1 exist? Why is it in the Bible? The reason why Genesis 1:1 exists is not an end in itself. It is a means to an end and the end is not that you would admit that you are made or even that God made you. Genesis was written to the people of God. It was written as part of a covenantal document. It was written to show the ancient people of God where they fit in God's purposes on earth. Notice that after Genesis 11, the narrative from chapters 12-50 focuses on Abraham, Isaac, Jacob, and Joseph. Why is that? Because Abraham, Isaac, Jacob, and Joseph are early participants in God's drama of redemption. God revealed the fact of initial creation to the ancient people in order to set the context for redemption. This implies that what was initially created changed. Something happened. And that something we call the fall into sin. Adam sinned and fell from his lofty state of existence in which he found himself as created. He was, as Luke 3:38 tells us, the first son of God on the earth. But he violated the law of God and death came to him and the rest of us. Genesis 1:1 exists to remind us that God made all things

---

[6] Muller, *Dictionary*, 251.

good so that the rupture that sin brings might be seen for what it is—
the creature's revolt against God which brings misery upon us all.

Through Moses God tells us that He made everything good, in
order that sin would be seen for what it is and in order that we might
understand why a rescue mission is needed. That rescue mission is
why the Bible exists. Listen to Hebrews 1:1-3.

> [1] God, after He spoke long ago to the fathers in the prophets in
> many portions and in many ways, [2] in these last days has spoken to
> us in His Son, whom He appointed heir of all things, through
> whom also He made the world. [3] And He is the radiance of His
> glory and the exact representation of His nature, and upholds all
> things by the word of His power. When He had made purification
> of sins, He sat down at the right hand of the Majesty on high,
> (Heb. 1:1-3)

Listen to 1 Corinthians 15:22, "For as in Adam all die, so also in
Christ all will be made alive." Speaking of Christ, Hebrews 2:10
says, "For it was fitting for Him, for whom are all things, and
through whom are all things, in bringing many sons to glory, to
perfect the author of their salvation through sufferings." The author
of creation is the triune God. The author of salvation is Jesus Christ,
who suffered the wrath of God to bring many sons to glory.

Evolutionist Richard Dawkins once said, "We are survival
machines—robot vehicles blindly programmed to preserve the selfish
molecules [of DNA] known as genes."[7] How depressing! No
wonder much of our pop-culture propagates a hopeless, meaningless
worldview which causes its adherents not to care about anything that
is worth caring about. It promotes a self-centered approach to life. It
produces me-oriented living. It produces people and whole societies
who are clueless and careless. In contrast, the Bible asserts that we
are creatures, created in God's image, fallen in sin, and in need of
salvation from sin's consequences. It also teaches that God has
provided salvation in the Son of God who became man for us and
for our salvation.

---

[7] Johnson, *Defeating Darwinism*, 69-70.

Brief Interaction with Those who Differ

Naturalistic evolution basically teaches that nobody times nothing equals everything. Naturalistic evolutionists advocate the evolution of all that we see through a natural process devoid of God. In 1995, the American National Association of Biology Teachers made this statement:

> The diversity of life on earth is the outcome of evolution: an unsupervised, impersonal, unpredictable and natural process of temporal descent with genetic modification that is affected by natural selection, chance, historical contingencies and changing environments.[8]

Nature is all there is. Matter (particles which make up matter and energy) is all there is. Evolutionist George Gaylord Simpson put it this way, "Man is the result of a purposeless and natural process that did not have him in mind."[9]

Some recent naturalistic evolutionists have admitted that matter is not all there is. They have been forced to admit that there is more to the natural world than physical things. So they have admitted that nature is comprised of both matter and what they call "information," such as DNA, numerical values, thoughts, feelings, and emotions. Just where this "information" came from, how it got here, how it could exist in a natural world of impersonal matter, how it could evolve from brute things is not known. But, that "information" exists, they cannot deny.

The Bible unashamedly asserts that God made everything there is that exists, excluding Himself, of course. The Christian is able to account for the heavens, the earth, man, animals, and "information." The Christian is even able to account for naturalistic evolution,

---

[8] Johnson, *Defeating Darwinism*, 15. It is fair to the American National Association of Biology Teachers to mention that this statement was amended after the publication of Johnson's book. See Johnson's discussion of the amended statement on pages 120-21.

[9] Johnson, *Defeating Darwinsim*, 15.

materialism, empiricism, and all other theories about origins and knowledge theory. These alternative theories to the biblical view exist because man is no longer what he was when he came from his maker's hand. Our ability to interpret the world around us and even our own souls has been distorted by the polluting, confusing power of sin. It is a disease we all share. It is destructive. It is deceiving. However, the Christian worldview has a solution to our problem. That solution is the gospel of our Lord Jesus Christ.

Chapter 7

The Six Days of Creation:
Creation "in the space of six days"

There is an important distinction we must make when we ask the question about the length of the days of creation. We must carefully distinguish between what we are and are not asking. We are not asking how long it took God to create the world, as if the job of creation demanded a certain time-frame due to the limitations in His ability to create. We are not talking about a being like us. We have power limitations. At some point, fatigue kicks in and we are forced to rest due to exhaustion. That is us, but that is not God. God did not take the time He took to create the heavens and the earth because He could not have done it faster. When a builder contracts with someone to build their home, the contract usually specifies a time-frame based on various factors. Being human, we have limitations of strength, for instance. We get tired. We need to be rejuvenated. We need sleep. Not so with God. "...the everlasting God, the LORD, the Creator of the ends of the earth, neither faints nor is weary" (Isa. 40:28). So we are not asking how long it took God to create the world.

What we are asking is this: How long did God take to create the world? That is a different question. Framing the question this way assumes that God could have taken as long as He wanted to create the heavens and the earth. Due to being omnipotent (all-powerful), omniscient (all-knowing and all-wise), if God thought it would have been wisest to create the world over billions and billions of years, He could certainly have done that.

But a further question is this: Why did God take however long He took to create the heavens and the earth? Does the Bible tell us, not only how long God took to create, but why He took that long? The answer is yes to both questions. We will pursue these below.

Views on the Length of the Days of Creation

As some readers are aware, there are various views on the issue of the duration of the days of creation vying for attention in our day. I will not critique them in this chapter. I will mention some of those views so readers are aware what is out there.

Some view the days of creation as long periods of time. No one knows how long, they say, but it is a long period of time–millions, and possibly billions, of years. God did not create in the space of six, twenty-four hour, days.

Others see Genesis 1 and 2 not as a narrative of what happened, but as a literary device through which Moses was affirming that God created everything. Moses does not indicate how long God took to do so. He could have created in the space of six, twenty-four hour, days but probably did not. No one can be sure but God alone. The point of the text is that Israel's God is creator.

The view I will be defending is stated in the Confession of Faith this way:

> In the beginning it pleased God the Father, Son, and Holy Spirit, for the manifestation of the glory of his eternal power, wisdom, and goodness, to Create or make the world, and all things therein, whether visible or invisible, in the space of six days, and all very good" (BCF 1689, 4.1).

I understand the confessional language to mean that God took six, twenty-four hour, days "to Create or make the world, and all things therein…"

Duration of the Six Days of Creation

The fact of six, twenty-four hour, days seems clear for various reasons. Here are some of them. The arguments should be considered as a whole, each one building upon and assuming the other. The arguments as formulated below are highly dependent upon both Louis Berkhof and Robert L. Reymond.[1]

"day"

There has been much discussion concerning the word "day" found in Genesis 1. Below are some of the reasons it should be taken to mean a normal twenty-four hour period of time.

> The word "day" (...*yom*), in the singular, dual and plural, occurs some 2,225 times in the Old Testament with the overwhelming preponderance of these occurrences designating the ordinary daily cycle. Normally, the preponderate meaning of a term should be maintained unless contextual considerations force one to another view.[2]

Berkhof adds, "[I]t is a good rule in exegesis, not to depart from the primary meaning of a word, unless this is required by the context."[3] There are no compelling reasons in Genesis 1 to understand the word "day" when referring to each of the six days of creation in any other way than the ordinary daily cycle, which is twenty-four hours in length.

"and there was evening and there was morning"

These words, or something very similar, occur in Genesis 1:5, 8, 13, 19, 23, and 31. In each instance, they indicate that God finished His work of creation for a particular day. Reymond says:

---

[1] Other helpful treatments of this issue can be found in Douglas Kelly, *Creation and Change*, 95-118 and Morton H. Smith, *Systematic Theology*, Volume I (Greenville, SC: Greenville Seminary Press, 1994), 187-88.

[2] Robert L. Reymond, *A New Systematic Theology of the Christian Faith* (Nashville: Thomas Nelson Publishers, 1998), 393.

[3] Louis Berkhof, *Systematic Theology* (Reprinted, May 1986; Grand Rapids: Wm. B. Eerdmans Publishing Co., 1939, 1941), 154.

The recurring phrase, "and the evening and the morning [taken together] constituted day one, etc." (1:5, 8, 13, 19, 23, 31). The qualifying words, "evening and morning," attached here to each of these recurring statements occur together outside of Genesis in 37 verses (e.g., Exod. 18:13; 27:21). In each instance these words are employed to describe an ordinary day.[4]

Berkhof adds, "Each of the days mentioned has just one evening and morning, something that would hardly apply to a period of thousands of years."[5]

"day" and ordinal numbers in the Old Testament

The universal testimony of the Old Testament when it uses "day" with ordinal numbers is that it refers to ordinary days. Reymond says:

> In the hundreds of other cases in the Old Testament where ... *yom* ["day"] stands in conjunction with an ordinal number (first, second, third, etc.), e.g., Exodus 12:15; 24:16; Leviticus 12:3, it never means anything other than a normal, literal day.[6]

The sun "to rule the day" and the moon "to rule the night"

Reymond asserts:

> With the creation of the sun "to rule the day" and the moon "to rule the night" occurring on the fourth day (Gen. 1:16–18), days four through six would almost certainly have been ordinary days. This would suggest that the seventh would also have been an ordinary day. All this would suggest in turn, if we may assume that the earth was turning on its axis at that time, that days one through three would have been ordinary days as well.[7]

---

[4] Reymond, *A New Systematic Theology*, 393.

[5] Berkhof, *Systematic Theology*, 154.

[6] Reymond, *A New Systematic Theology*, 393.

[7] Reymond, *A New Systematic Theology*, 393-94. Cf. Berkhof, *Systematic Theology*, 155 and Smith, *Systematic Theology*, I:188.

Exodus 20 and the days of creation

Moses, the author of both Genesis and Exodus, alludes to the six days of creation as well as the seventh day, the Sabbath day at creation. In Exodus 20:8-11 we read:

> [8] "Remember the sabbath day, to keep it holy. [9] "Six days you shall labor and do all your work, [10] but the seventh day is a sabbath of the LORD your God; *in it* you shall not do any work, you or your son or your daughter, your male or your female servant or your cattle or your sojourner who stays with you. [11] "For in six days the LORD made the heavens and the earth, the sea and all that is in them, and rested on the seventh day; therefore the LORD blessed the sabbath day and made it holy. (Exod. 20:8-11)

This is an important biblical text because it provides a divine commentary on the days of creation. Reymond comments:

> [Allowing the Bible to look back and comment on the days of creation,] ...the "ordinary day" view has most to commend it since Moses grounds the commandment regarding seventh-day Sabbath observance in the fact of the divine Exemplar's activity: "In six days the Lord made the heavens and the earth, the sea, and all that is in them, but he rested on the seventh day. Therefore the LORD blessed the Sabbath day and made it holy" (Exod. 20:11; see also 31:15–17).[8]

Sam Waldron provides these helpful comments on Exodus 20:

> Jehovah insists that he made everything in exactly six days. This is a simple statement of historical fact. Further, if the seven-day structure of the creation week is mere literary frame-work, why does Jehovah himself attribute such significance to it? A related problem is that Jehovah identifies the seventh day of creation as a sabbath day. The second part of verse 11 is a quotation or paraphrase and thus is *an interpretation* [emphasis mine] of Gen. 2:3. The point of intense interest is that in Exodus 20:11 Jehovah

---

[8] Reymond, *A New Systematic Theology*, 394.

calls the seventh day of creation 'a sabbath day'. The meaning of 'sabbath day' in Exodus 20:11 may not be disputed. The sabbath day in this passage is a literal day. It means every recurring literal, seventh day of every week.[9]

The plural use of "days" in the Old Testament

In the 608 occurrences of the plural "days" [*yamim*] …in the Old Testament (see Exod. 20:11), their referents are always ordinary days. Ages are never expressed by the word …*yamim* ["days"].[10]

In Exodus 20:11, Moses wrote, "For in six days [note the plural use] the LORD made the heavens and the earth…"

The lack of "age" terminology

Finally, had Moses intended to express the idea of seven "ages" in Genesis 1, he could have employed the term …*olam*, which means "age" or "period of indeterminate duration."[11]

Taken together, the picture is clear. The triune God created the Son-tilted heavens and the earth for His own glory in the space of six, ordinary, twenty-four hour days.

Why in the Space of Six Days?

Why did God create in the space of six days? The reason is not to be found in anything necessary in the Persons of the Godhead or the nature and essence of God. God did not take six days to create because that is how much time it took Him due to strength or time or knowledge or wisdom constraints. In other words, it could have been done in another way, assuming it would have reflected God's

---

[9] Samuel E. Waldron, *A Modern Exposition of the 1689 Baptist Confession of Faith* (Reprint 2005; Darlington, England: Evangelical Press, 1989), 78.

[10] Reymond, *A New Systematic Theology*, 394.

[11] Reymond, *A New Systematic Theology*, 394.

wisdom, power, goodness, and purpose for creating in the first place, but it was not.

Why did God create in the space of six days? I think the reason is as follows. As we will see in the next chapter, the Mount Everest of creation is not the sun and moon, not the stars and the galaxies or even the earth itself. The Mount Everest of God's creation is man–male and female, created in His image. God took six days to create for us, male and female in the image of God. In other words, God did what He did for us to pattern ourselves after Him.[12] This is clear from Exodus 20:11 cited above.

Three Final Observations

Interpreting the Bible and the days of creation

The arguments above for my understanding of the length of creation days utilized Bible texts and patterns of expression found outside of Genesis 1. When asking a question about any text of Scripture, the safest place to go for answers is the Scripture itself. In the case of the days of creation, God speaks. He interprets them for us through the words of Moses in Exodus 20:11 (and in other places). This is the divine interpretation and therefore it is infallible–it cannot be wrong.[13] John Owen said many years ago:

> The only unique, public, authentic, and infallible interpreter of Scripture is none other than the Author of Scripture Himself, by whose inspiration they are the truth, and by whom they possess their perspicuity and authority, that is, God the Holy Spirit.[14]

The only infallible interpreter of Holy Scripture is the Holy Spirit in the Holy Scripture. This is a very safe hermeneutical rule. When the

---

[12] We will explore this concept of following the example of our maker in the next two chapters and in the chapters on the Sabbath Rest of Creation.

[13] Of course, my interpretation of the text could be wrong but God's can't.

[14] John Owen, *Biblical Theology* (Pittsburgh: Soli Deo Gloria Publications, 1994), 797.

Bible comments upon itself, it is God's commentary on God's Word. This interpretive principle is called *analogia Scripturae* (i.e., the analogy of Scripture). Richard Muller says this principle involves "the interpretation of unclear, difficult, or ambiguous passages of Scripture by comparison with clear and unambiguous passages *that refer to the same teaching or event*" (emphasis mine).[15] With reference to the days of creation, Exodus 20:11 is its divine commentary.

Some of the arguments utilized above employed another principle of interpretation called *analogia fidei* (i.e., the analogy of faith). This principle is broader than *analogia Scripturae*. It refers to

> the use of a general sense of the meaning of Scripture, constructed from the clear or unambiguous *loci* [i.e., places]..., as the basis for interpreting unclear or ambiguous texts. As distinct from the more basic *analogia Scripturae*..., the *analogia fidei* presupposes a sense of the theological meaning of Scripture.[16]

Both of these interpretive principles presuppose "the canonical character of the whole of Scripture and the assumption that the canon, as such, was inspired and the infallible rule of faith and practice..."[17]

There are at least two reasons why understanding the principles of interpretation mentioned and utilized above are important. It is important so the reader understands how I got to the conclusions to which I arrived. But it is also important to set the stage for subsequent discussions on the creation account and its implications. What does it mean to be created in the image of God? The text of Genesis 1:26 does not define what man *imago Dei* (i.e., in the image of God) is. What was Adam's assignment and does subsequent revelation look back on Eden and help us understand what that was?

---

[15] Muller, *Dictionary*, 33.

[16] Muller, *Dictionary*, 33.

[17] Richard A. Muller, *Post-Reformation Reformed Dogmatics: The Rise and Development of Reformed Orthodoxy, ca. 1520 to ca. 1725, Volume Two, Holy Scripture,* The Cognitive Foundation of Theology (Grand Rapids: Baker Academic, 2003, Second Edition), 474.

What does the Creator's rest or Sabbath mean with reference to God and us, if anything? These are important questions. You will notice in the chapters that follow that allowing the Bible its proper place in the interpretive process sheds much needed light on texts and passages that at first seem to be obscure. We will see that subsequent revelation often makes explicit what is only implicit in antecedent revelation.

Man imago Dei *and the days of creation*

As we will see in the next two chapters, being created in God's image has ethical implications. Because we are made in God's image, we are to reflect who He is and what He does, according to the created capacities with which we are endowed. As will be argued in subsequent chapters, the work/rest cycle of God established at creation was to be patterned by Adam. As God is holy, we are to be holy in both work and rest.[18] Since being made in God's image implies that He has ethical claims upon us, we are in a bond of accountability to our Creator. But, as we all know too well, not only did Adam sin and plunge the rest of mankind into moral guilt and pollution, the rest of us sin as well on a daily basis. "For all have sinned and fall short of the glory of God" (Rom. 3:23). Since God created us, we are accountable to be and do what He requires. And herein is everyone's problem. Since the fall into sin, no one does good, there is none righteous (cf. Rom. 3:10-12). Though we are still image-bearers of God and responsible to work and rest as He did, none of us do. This brings me to a third final observation for this chapter.

---

[18] We will discuss what Adam's work and rest means in subsequent chapters. At this juncture, it may help the reader to know that I will argue that Adam was a priest, responsible to build God's temple-kingdom starting in the garden of Eden and extending it to the four corners of the earth. Upon the successful completion of that work, Adam would have entered God's rest.

The gospel and the days of creation

Does the gospel relate to the days of creation? I think it does. God (the Father, Son, and Holy Spirit) created the heavens and the earth (and mankind) in the space of six days and then He rested, and all was very good (Gen. 1:31). However, it is not all very good now. The gospel is the good news that God the Creator did not leave the entirety of His creation to be damned and end in utter ruin. He put a rescue-plan in operation. He first reveals this plan in Genesis 3:15 in the context of cursing the serpent. "And I will put enmity Between you and the woman, And between your seed and her seed; He shall bruise you on the head, And you shall bruise him on the heel" (Gen. 3:15). Here is the promise of a skull-crushing seed of the woman who ends up destroying the works of the devil (1 John 3:8).

This promise ends up being fulfilled by the eternal Son of God, "the exact representation of [God's] nature" (Heb. 1:3), becoming one of us–He became man *imago Dei*. He did this in order to repair the damage done by sin. Jesus Christ did not sin on any day of the week. He obeyed, unlike Adam, working and resting without sin His entire life. But He did not obey simply as proof of His unique identity. The eternal Son of God obeyed in human nature on behalf of others. Christ's perfect, weekly obedience is the ground upon which believing sinners are pronounced righteous in God's sight. And some day, He will usher those who believe in Him into the "new heavens and a new earth, in which righteousness dwells" (2 Pet. 3:13). Believers will enter God's rest (Heb. 4). Creation and new creation are vitally related in the biblical drama of revelation. Redemption by Christ is connected to creation in the space of six days.

Chapter 8

The Image-Bearing Apex of Creation (I):
Creation in the image of God

So far, it has been argued that God made all things for His own glory. The triune God–Father, Son, and Holy Spirit–fashioned all created things in a Son-tilted manner. All that has been made tells of His glory and testifies of His existence. The act of creation by the triune God was an *ex nihilo* act, creation out of nothing. And finally, God made all things in the space of six days. He did so as a pattern for us to follow. The next two chapters address the creation of man, the image-bearing apex of creation.

What is man? This is a very important question. If we do not know who we are, we will not know what we are supposed to do. If we are part of an impersonal system of the survival of the fittest, then our job is to survive and to exterminate anything or anyone who gets in our way. If evolution is true, man is nothing but an advanced beast, the product of an unceasing, impersonal process that weeds out inferior beings. Knowing where we come from not only tells us "how we got here, [but] why we are like we are, who is in charge, by whose rules we should play, and by whose rules we will be judged."[1] This is an important issue. The Bible is clear: God made man in His image, requires man to live in light of that image, and will hold man accountable for how he lives.

In this chapter, we will focus our attention on the creation of man, the image-bearing apex of creation. By apex I mean the summit, the climax, or as was said in previous discussion, the Mount Everest of creation.

---

[1] Kelly, *Creation and Change*, 17.

High-Level Observations Indicating that Man is the Apex of Creation

In Genesis 1:3, 6, 9, 11, 14, 20, and 24 the words, "Then God said" occur. In each instance, they are followed by the words, "Let there be" or something similar to it. However, in Genesis 1:26, after the words, "Then God said" occur these words, "Let Us make." Something is unique about man. From Genesis 2:4 onward, though aspects of the initial creation are repeated, the focus is on man (2:7, 8, 15-25). Something is unique about man. In Genesis 5, where we have a genealogy that ends with Noah, the beginning of it reminds us of the creation of man (Gen. 5:1-2). In Genesis 9, the covenant with Noah, God reminds Noah of man's creation (Gen. 9:6). Again, something is unique about man.

The most alarming and mysterious teaching of the Bible about the uniqueness of man, however, is found in the New Testament. Listen to these texts.

> [1] In the beginning was the Word, and the Word was with God, and the Word was God. [2] He was in the beginning with God. [3] All things came into being through Him, and apart from Him nothing came into being that has come into being. [4] In Him was life, and the life was the Light of men. [5] The Light shines in the darkness, and the darkness did not comprehend it. (John 1:1-5)

> And the Word became flesh, and dwelt among us, and we saw His glory, glory as of the only begotten from the Father, full of grace and truth. (John 1:14)

> For you know the grace of our Lord Jesus Christ, that though He was rich, yet for your sake He became poor, so that you through His poverty might become rich. (2Cor. 8:9)

> But when the fullness of the time came, God sent forth His Son, born of a woman, born under the Law, (Gal. 4:4)

> [5] Have this attitude in yourselves which was also in Christ Jesus, [6] who, although He existed in the form of God, did not regard

equality with God a thing to be grasped, [7] but emptied Himself, taking the form of a bond-servant, *and* being made in the likeness of men. [8] Being found in appearance as a man, He humbled Himself by becoming obedient to the point of death, even death on a cross. (Phil. 2:5-8)

For in Him all the fullness of Deity dwells in bodily form, (Col. 2:9)

[14] Therefore, since the children share in flesh and blood, He Himself likewise also partook of the same, that through death He might render powerless him who had the power of death, that is, the devil, [15] and might free those who through fear of death were subject to slavery all their lives. [16] For assuredly He does not give help to angels, but He gives help to the descendant of Abraham. [17] Therefore, He had to be made like His brethren in all things, so that He might become a merciful and faithful high priest in things pertaining to God, to make propitiation for the sins of the people. [18] For since He Himself was tempted in that which He has suffered, He is able to come to the aid of those who are tempted. (Heb. 2:14-18)

[5] Therefore, when He comes into the world, He says, "SACRIFICE AND OFFERING YOU HAVE NOT DESIRED, BUT A BODY YOU HAVE PREPARED FOR ME; [6] IN WHOLE BURNT OFFERINGS AND *sacrifices* FOR SIN YOU HAVE TAKEN NO PLEASURE. [7] "THEN I SAID, 'BEHOLD, I HAVE COME (IN THE SCROLL OF THE BOOK IT IS WRITTEN OF ME) TO DO YOUR WILL, O GOD.'" [8] After saying above, "SACRIFICES AND OFFERINGS AND WHOLE BURNT OFFERINGS AND *sacrifices* FOR SIN YOU HAVE NOT DESIRED, NOR HAVE YOU TAKEN PLEASURE *in them*" (which are offered according to the Law), [9] then He said, "BEHOLD, I HAVE COME TO DO YOUR WILL." He takes away the first in order to establish the second. [10] By this will we have been sanctified through the offering of the body of Jesus Christ once for all. (Heb. 10:5-10)

By common confession, great is the mystery of godliness: He who was revealed in the flesh, Was vindicated in the Spirit, Seen by angels, Proclaimed among the nations, Believed on in the world, Taken up in glory. (1 Tim. 3:16)

For God so loved the world, that He gave His only begotten Son, that whoever believes in Him shall not perish, but have eternal life. (John 3:16)

Why did God send His Son to become man? Why such condescension? Why become one of us? What is man to be given such love, such mercy, such grace? What a strange design. There must be something about man that God is vitally interested in. But what is it? It is the fact that man was created in the image of God and is, therefore, the apex of creation. God loves His image so much He became one of us to repair it and bring it to glory. Hear John Owen:

...what heart can conceive, what tongue can express, the glory of that condescension in the Son of God, whereby he took our nature upon him, took it to be his own, in order unto a discharge of the office of mediation on our behalf?[2]

Charles Wesley's hymn, "And can it be?," captures the amazing, mysterious, condescending grace of God in the incarnation of the Son well.

He left His Father's throne above (So free, so infinite His grace!) Humbled Himself because of love, And bled for all His chosen race: Tis mercy all, immense and free; For O my God, it found out me.[3]

---

[2] John Owen, *The Works of John Owen,* Volume I (Edinburgh, Scotland and Carlisle, PA: The Banner of Truth Trust, Reprinted 1987), 325.

[3] *Trinity Hymnal,* hymn #731:3.

Exegetical and Theological Considerations Indicating that Man is the Apex of Creation

The divine announcement of man's creation: "Let Us..."

There are at least three views explaining the plural "Us."[4] Some see "Us" as referring to a heavenly court, inclusive of the angels. However, angels did not create; God did. Also, "Our image" and "Our likeness" is further described for us in the next verse as "God created man in His own image." And if that's not clear enough, Moses adds, "in the image of God He created him; male and female He created them." God is clearly the exclusive creator, not a heavenly court inclusive of angels.

Others see "Us" as a plural of majesty, noting that in the ancient world kings used to speak of themselves in the plural, seeking to engender respect from their subjects. However, it has been shown by scholars of the ancient world that the plural of majesty was introduced by the Persians long after Moses wrote Genesis.[5]

The third view understands this verse as a rudimentary or not fully-developed reference to the Trinity–the three distinct Persons of the Godhead all sharing the one, entire essence of divinity or deity. We have already seen that the Bible is clear–the Father, the Son of God, and the Spirit of God all played a part in the act of creation. Interestingly, Genesis 1:2 mentions the function of the Spirit of God in creation. Some shy away from this view claiming that the original readers would not have known that. However, we are not interested in speculating about how the original readers understood this.[6] The Scripture, which is our only infallible guide, is clear that each Person of the Godhead executed divine power in the creation of all things. I think this view is correct and it is the more commonly held view over the centuries. What we have here is an intra-Trinitarian, executive divine counsel.[7] Here is a vague hint at something the rest

---

[4] Cf. Fesko, *Last Things First*, 40-45.
[5] Cf. Fesko, *Last things First*, 44.
[6] Cf. Fesko, *Last things First*, 45.
[7] Kelly, *Creation and Change*, 193.

of the Bible unfolds and the church recognized over time: "there is a richness of interpersonal life within the Godhead, which Christians came to call 'the Trinity.'"[8]

The superlative action in man's creation

Three times in Genesis 1:27 Moses uses the verb "created" and each time God is the subject, the Creator, and man is the object, that which was created. "God created man in His own image, in the image of God He created him; male and female He created them" (Gen. 1:27). Why is this? Does he think we can't read? And why is this three-fold use of the word only used in the creation of man? Fesko says, "The repetition most likely indicates the superlative, namely, that man is the apex of God's creation."[9] Moses could have said it once, but he repeats himself. The repetition highlights the uniqueness of man. It points to the fact that though God made the heavens and the earth, the sea, the land, the stars, the sun, the moon, plants, and animals, man is unique, man is special, man is something different than all the rest of God's creation.

The exclusive terminology of man's creation

Genesis 1:26-27 says:

> [26] Then God said, "Let Us make man in Our image, according to Our likeness; and let them rule over the fish of the sea and over the birds of the sky and over the cattle and over all the earth, and over every creeping thing that creeps on the earth." [27] God created man in His own image, in the image of God He created him; male and female He created them. (Gen. 1:26-27)

Notice the exclusive terminology–"Our image…Our likeness…His own image…the image of God." No other aspect of creation is so designated. Whatever this means, we know this much: man is the

---

[8] Kelly, *Creation and Change*, 193.
[9] Fesko, *Last Things First*, 51.

apex of God's creation. God takes special counsel in his creation and He makes man in His own image, to reflect Him on the earth, to be like Him in ways no other creation of God is able.

What constitutes man so unique, so privileged, so different than all other created entities is the fact that he alone is created in God's image. Though everything that is, outside of God, was created by God, man is the apex, the pinnacle, the Mount Everest of what He has made. This is so due to man's creation–male and female–in the image of God. But what does this mean?

Notice the terminology of man created in God's image. Moses says, "Then God said, 'Let Us make man in Our image, according to Our likeness...'" (Gen. 1:26a). In the next verse, he says, "God created man in His own image, in the image of God He created him; male and female He created them" (Gen. 1:27) Notice how in verse 27 the word "likeness" is not used. Verse 26 says, "...Our image, ...Our likeness..." In Genesis 5:1-2, Moses refers back to man's creation.

[1] This is the book of the generations of Adam. In the day when God created man, He made him in the likeness of God. [2] He created them male and female, and He blessed them and named them Man in the day when they were created. (Gen. 5:1-2)

Moses does not use the word "image" here. In Genesis 9:6, he uses "image" and not "likeness." "Whoever sheds man's blood, By man his blood shall be shed, For in the image of God He made man" (Gen. 9:6). Paul uses the term "image" to refer to creation in 1 Corinthians 11:7a. "For a man ought not to have his head covered, since he is the image and glory of God..." (1 Cor. 11:7a). In this text, whatever "image of God" means it is what man *is* not what man *possesses*. And notice that Paul does not use the term "likeness." James 3:9 says, "With it [our tongue] we bless *our* Lord and Father, and with it we curse men, who have been made in the likeness of God" (James 3:9). Notice that James says "likeness" and does not use the word "image." Also, this text indicates that man, even after the fall into sin, is still the "likeness" of God.

This interchange of the terms "image" and "likeness" indicates that they are basically synonymous terms.[10] Whatever it means to be the image of God, being the likeness of God means the same thing.

The meaning of man's creation in the image of God

The fact of man's creation in the image of God argues for man as the apex of creation. But what does it mean to be created in God's image? There are at least three ways one could seek to define creation in God's image. The first is to go to Genesis 1:26-27, identify the terms which describe man as created, then consult a dictionary to determine the meaning of those words. Once the dictionary definition is found it would be applied to the text. But both words in this case (i.e., "image" and "likeness") mean basically the same thing. Man is like God in some sense due to how he has been made.

A second way would be to go to other texts that use the same words. However, we would find the same thing–both words mean basically the same thing.

A third way would be to go to texts that explain what these terms mean or what they imply. This third way is the best method because it allows God to tell us what these terms mean. Let us apply this method of investigation in order to determine the meaning of these terms. We will look at several texts that end up giving us the Bible's explanation of what it means to be created in God's image.

Our first text is Ecclesiastes 7:29, which says, "Behold, I have found only this, that God made men upright, but they have sought out many devices." This could mean that God made man physically "upright." Man at creation took his first breath standing. However, this would mean that seeking "out many devices" would refer to the many ways since man's creation that he seeks not to be physically upright. The author is contrasting being made upright with seeking out many devices. Though it is true that since man's creation he has sought out many ways of not being physically upright, there is not

---

[10] Herman Bavinck, Louis Berkhof, Douglas F. Kelly, and J. V. Fesko take this view.

anything inherently wrong with that. The author of these words is not talking about physical uprightness since there is nothing wrong with crawling or lying down, for instance. It is best to understand this as referring to man's original moral uprightness. Man was originally holy. He had integrity of soul. The devices we all seek are sinful devices, sinful ways. This seeking "out many devices" is wrong. It is not in accord with man's original state of integrity. Man was made morally upright but something happened. Creation *imago Dei* included moral integrity.

Colossians 3:10 is another text that sheds light on being created *imago Dei*. That text reads, "and have put on the new self who is being renewed to a true knowledge according to the image of the One who created him." It is important to note that Paul is talking about believers in Christ in this passage. Specifically, he is talking about the work of the renovation of man by God or, as the older writers put it, the work of the reparation of human nature. "Being renewed" may be translated "being renovated" or "repaired." This work of renovation involves "being renewed to a true knowledge." Something is wrong with our minds. They have been stained by sin. They need renovation by the Spirit of God to a true knowledge of God.

Notice that this work of renovation, or reparation, is "according to the image of the One who created him." It is a renovation in which believers are made to be like God, according to His image, with reference to their minds, and in accordance with how God made man in the beginning. So Adam and Eve were given the true knowledge of God at their creation and believers in Christ have that true knowledge restored, "according to the image of the One who created him."

Ephesians 4:24 is a similar text. It says, "and put on the new self, which in *the likeness of* God has been created in righteousness and holiness of the truth." As in Colossians, Paul is talking about believers in Christ. He is talking about the work of the renovation of man. This work of renovation, or reparation, is "in *the likeness of* God" or literally "according to God." It is a renovation in which believers are made to be like God in a way they were not prior to being renovated. This implies that unbelievers are not like God in this sense. This work of renovation involves a creation–"…has been created…" I do not think this refers to the initial creation. Paul is dealing with what he calls "a new creation" in 2 Corinthians 5:17, "Therefore if anyone is in Christ, *he is* a new creature ["creation" in many versions]; the old things passed away; behold, new things have come." Being a part of this new creation has to do with one's relationship to Christ. This work of renovation involves being "created in righteousness and holiness of the truth." To be righteous means to be rightly related to God due to being rightly related to God's law. To be holy means to be pure of mind, heart, and will. Man was made righteous and holy. He was morally pure.

Being the image of God for Adam, then, meant that his mind was stocked with and able to process true knowledge of God. His heart was morally pure; he was made upright. His will acted in accordance with the law of God. Romans 2:14-15 teaches us that all men have the law of God written on their hearts due to being created. This was certainly true of the first man, Adam. The Confession puts it this way:

> After God had made all other creatures, he created man, male and female, …being made after the image of God, in knowledge, righteousness, and true holiness; having the law of God written in their hearts, and power to fulfil it" (BCF 1689, 4.2)

Brief Excursus on Man's Body and God's Image

What about man's body? Man's body takes up space. It is a material entity. Genesis 2:7 implies that man is comprised of matter and that which is not matter. "Then the LORD God formed man of dust from the ground, and breathed into his nostrils the breath of life; and man became a living being" (Gen. 2:7). That which comes from the dust is called man and it was into man that the LORD God breathed the breath of life. Man's being, that which constitutes him what he is essentially, includes a material and an immaterial aspect. So man–body and soul–is the image of God. But, someone says, "Jesus said, 'God is Spirit' (John 4:24). How can man's body be created in the image of God if God does not have a body like men, as *The Children's Catechism* says. This seems to be a contradiction. Isn't it better to say that man's soul, and not his body, is what constitutes him as being created in the image of God?" How do we sort through this?

Just as the creation, the heavens, "tell of His glory" (Psa. 19:1) and just as "His invisible attributes, His eternal power and divine nature, have been clearly seen, being understood through what has been made…" (Rom. 1:20), so with man's body. It is a created conduit through which man is God's image on the earth. Herman Bavinck says, "All creatures are embodiments of divine thoughts, and all of them display the footsteps or vestiges of God."[11] This applies to our bodies as well. The image of God is what man is not what man ought to be. Do we look at a sunset and say, "Since the sun reflects the power and wisdom of God, since it tells of His glory and displays before us His invisible attributes, His power and divine nature, and since the sun is a material or physical creation of God, God is, therefore, material or physical"? The answer is no. The sun is a created means through which the unseen God makes Himself known to His creatures. We do not look at a beautiful tree and conclude that God must be a tree, or a physical entity which takes up space. The same goes for our bodies. We do not look at our bodies and conclude that God must have a body like men, at least we should not. Our bodies are created conduits through which the power of our soul is exerted. Being created in the image of God does not tell us so much about God, as it tells us about ourselves.[12] We were made to represent God on the earth, unlike any other creature. We were given souls and bodies to do this, but this does not mean that God has a soul and God has a body like man. That which has been made in the image of God does not make God like the image that He made.

---

[11] Herman Bavinck, *Reformed Dogmatics: God and Creation*, II, translated by John Vriend (Grand Rapids: Baker Academic, 2008), 561, see Ibid., 531 for a similar statement.

[12] Bavinck, *Reformed Dogmatics,* II:533.

Some Implications of Man Created
in the Image of God

Though man is not God, man is God's creation, in His image,
which means that God has claims upon us.

Several years ago, I was told on the basketball court, "Preacher, it's
your universe, you create." I corrected the theology of my teammate
immediately. "It's not my universe and I do not have the power or
authority to create." In our day, you often hear things like, "It's her
body. She may do what she wants with it. If she thinks a baby will
be too much of an inconvenience at this time of her life, there are
ways to preserve her convenience." However, body and soul, we
belong to God. These things are gifts that we are stewards of, not the
basis for doing as we please with them. Remember, the universe
exists because God called it into being for His glory (Rom. 11:36).
He does not give us the right to act as if He does not exist. There is a
law of God which is intrinsic to our being (Rom. 2:14ff.). It comes
with the territory of who we are. It is according to this law that we
are accountable to God. Understanding what it means to be created
in the image of God makes this clear. Being His image means that
we are accountable to Him.

This perspective on man as God's image is the foundation upon
which capital punishment for murder was instituted by God.

"Whoever sheds man's blood, By man his blood shall be shed, For
in the image of God He made man" (Gen. 9:6). Why would God
give man the authority to take the life of a murderer? The answer
lies in the fact that man represents God on the earth, like no other
creature. Man has judicial authority on the earth bestowed upon him
by God due to his status as the image of God. Murder is an act in
which an image of God is destroyed in a manner forbidden by God–
"thou shalt not murder." "Vengeance is mine, says the LORD" (Deut.
32:35; Rom. 12:19). Only God has the right to kill and make alive (1
Sam. 2:6) and He does this every day. However, God has given man

the authority to take the life of murderers to satisfy His temporal justice and to teach the murderer and the rest of us that creation *imago Dei* is a big deal to Him.

Being created in the image of God, Adam and Eve had true knowledge of God, were morally upright, and loved His law.

This is clear from the discussion above. But what happened? Is it the case that all men and women today have true knowledge of God, are morally upright and pure of heart, and love His law? It does not take much thought to conclude, "No." In fact, the Bible asserts, in many places, that our minds are futile, our hearts are polluted, and that there is none righteous because our wills are bound to sin (John 6:44; Rom. 1:18-32; 3:10-12; 8:17; Eph. 2:1-3; 4:17-19). When Adam and Eve sinned, human nature was scared, marred, shattered, twisted, distorted, mangled, and made unfit to be what it was made to be. Something is way wrong with us.

This understanding of the image of God and man's fall into sin explains all the sorrow and pain experienced all over the world every day.

It explains all the heartaches, all the troubles, all the wars, all the violence, all the lying, cheating, stealing, adultery, fornication of various sorts, hatred, and idolatry throughout man's history. We are not in the same condition in which we were made, "for all have sinned and fall short of the glory of God" (Rom. 3:23). We have all sought out many devices (Eccl. 7:29). We need help and we are unable to provide it for ourselves. We need to be repaired. We need renovation. We need a permanent fix to our current problem.

Though man had a good start in the garden of Eden, things have changed drastically since then. Adam sinned and his sin affected everyone (Rom. 5:12-21). The entire human race was plunged into a deformed state of existence. Death came as a result of sin. Curse came as a result of sin. Distortion and discordance came as a result of sin. Disorder came as a result of sin. Confusion came as a result of sin. The image-bearing apex of creation brought catastrophic change into the arena of the world due to sin. And what did God do? He banished Adam and Eve from the garden (Gen. 3:23), He exiled them. He pronounced judgment upon them and the serpent (Gen. 3:13-19). Adam and Eve were kicked out of God's Edenic house. A dramatic event occurred early in man's history that has infected us all.

This understanding of the image of God sheds light on the glorious news of the gospel.

The drama does not stop with exile from God's favorable presence. The chilling account of man's banishment from the special presence and favor of God in the garden of Eden, man's loss of communion with God, and his loss of righteousness, is not the end of the story. In the midst of this dark scene of God's curse, a ray of hope and promise emerges in a most peculiar manner. God says this to the serpent, "And I will put enmity Between you and the woman, And between your seed and her seed; He shall bruise you on the head, And you shall bruise him on the heel" (Gen. 3:15). In this judgment upon the serpent there lies a promise, a glimmer of hope for the future. One born of a woman will come and destroy the works of the devil (1 John 3:8). That one will win the day. That one will rescue the image of God which was shattered, marred, and scared by the fall into sin. Paul says, "Now the promises were spoken to Abraham and to his seed. He does not say, 'And to seeds,' as referring to many, but rather to one, 'And to your seed,' that is, Christ" (Gal. 3:16) and "But when the fullness of the time came, God sent forth His Son, born of a woman, born under the Law, so that He might redeem those who were under the Law, that we might receive the adoption as sons..." (Gal. 4:4-5). John says, "The Son of God appeared for this purpose, to destroy the works of the devil" (1 John 3:8b). And then there is Hebrews 2:10-18.

[10] For it was fitting for Him, for whom are all things, and through whom are all things, in bringing many sons to glory, to perfect the author of their salvation through sufferings. [11] For both He who

sanctifies and those who are sanctified are all from one *Father*; for which reason He is not ashamed to call them brethren, [12] saying, "I WILL PROCLAIM YOUR NAME TO MY BRETHREN, IN THE MIDST OF THE CONGREGATION I WILL SING YOUR PRAISE." [13] And again, "I WILL PUT MY TRUST IN HIM." And again, "BEHOLD, I AND THE CHILDREN WHOM GOD HAS GIVEN ME." [14] Therefore, since the children share in flesh and blood, He Himself likewise also partook of the same, that through death He might render powerless him who had the power of death, that is, the devil, [15] and might free those who through fear of death were subject to slavery all their lives. [16] For assuredly He does not give help to angels, but He gives help to the descendant of Abraham. [17] Therefore, He had to be made like His brethren in all things, so that He might become a merciful and faithful high priest in things pertaining to God, to make propitiation for the sins of the people. [18] For since He Himself was tempted in that which He has suffered, He is able to come to the aid of those who are tempted.

The Son of God became man that He might suffer for us and bring many sons to glory. God loved His image so much the Son of God was sent to assume human nature in order to bring many sons to glory. This is, indeed, good news.

Chapter 9

The Image-Bearing Apex of Creation (II):
Creation in the image of God

In the last chapter, it was argued that man was made morally upright, he was holy, and had integrity of soul (Eccl. 7:29). Though we are not what Adam and Eve were at creation, when they were created, they had moral integrity. Man at creation possessed true knowledge of God (Col. 3:10). Adam and Eve knew God rightly. They did not suppress the truths about God testified by the creation like we do. Finally, man was created in righteousness and holiness of the truth (Eph. 4:24). He had the law written on his heart (Rom. 2:14ff.). He was rightly related to God because rightly related to His law. His holiness, his moral purity, lined up with the truth of God's law.

Man was created to reflect who God is and what He does more than any other aspect of God's creation. Man, and man alone, was created in the image of God. That is why Adam's sin, Adam's failure to be a good image of God, has such radical consequences. It affected Adam, Eve, and all their children since. In fact, if Adam was faithful, there would be no sin, no death, no hell for man, no need for salvation, and no need for a Bible. But, as we know too well, something catastrophic happened. A massive rupture between God and man occurred. Adam sinned; he transgressed God's law—first, in his heart and then with his actions. Moral pollution entered his soul and death came upon all. All the troubles, trials, and tragedies in the world today are the result of that first sin. Sin ruptured the relationship man had with God and man was expelled from the paradise into which God put him. Now we live in a wilderness of sin and sorrow, of trials and troubles, of doom and death. Man fell from a lofty state.

The question we will be pursuing in this chapter is: What did God give Adam and Eve to do and what is God's response to their failure? Man's calling was the highest calling of all of God's earthly creatures being created in the image of God. But just what was Adam to do as God's image and what was God's response to man's failure?

The way we will approach this question is to make observations about Adam's identity and calling, then look at God's remedy for his failure. We will focus primarily on Adam due to Paul's words in Romans 5:12-19.

> [12] Therefore, just as through one man sin entered into the world, and death through sin, and so death spread to all men, because all sinned-- [13] for until the Law sin was in the world, but sin is not imputed when there is no law. [14] Nevertheless death reigned from Adam until Moses, even over those who had not sinned in the likeness of the offense of Adam, who is a type of Him who was to come. [15] But the free gift is not like the transgression. For if by the transgression of the one the many died, much more did the grace of God and the gift by the grace of the one Man, Jesus Christ, abound to the many. [16] The gift is not like *that which came* through the one who sinned; for on the one hand the judgment *arose* from one *transgression* resulting in condemnation, but on the other hand the free gift *arose* from many transgressions resulting in justification. [17] For if by the transgression of the one, death reigned through the one, much more those who receive the abundance of grace and of the gift of righteousness will reign in life through the One, Jesus Christ. [18] So then as through one transgression there resulted condemnation to all men, even so through one act of righteousness there resulted justification of life to all men. [19] For as through the one man's disobedience the many were made sinners, even so through the obedience of the One the many will be made righteous. (Rom. 5:12-19)

Adam was a public person. He stood as a representative of others. As he went, so went the rest of us. This is important to understand in order to understand Adam's vocation. It is also crucial to understand the vocation of our Lord Jesus Christ.

Observations upon Adam's Identity and Calling

Adam was an image-bearer, which placed ethical demands upon him.

"Then God said, 'Let Us make man in Our image, according to Our likeness; ...' [27] "God created man in His own image, in the image of God He created him; male and female He created them" (Gen. 1:26-27). As stated above, this has ethical implications for man's conduct. Adam was to be like God according the abilities with which he was endowed at his creation. As Meredith G. Kline says:

> Man's likeness to God is a demand to be like God; the indicative here has the force of an imperative. Formed in the image of God, man is informed by a sense of deity by which he knows what God is like, not merely that God is (Rom 1:19ff.).[1]

Man's sense of the divine has ethical implications.

Adam was sinless.

"Behold, I have found only this, that God made men upright, but they have sought out many devices" (Eccl. 7:29). Adam possessed moral integrity as a direct result of creation. The justice of God had no claims on him.

Adam was told to be fruitful and multiply, and fill the earth, and subdue it.

"God blessed them; and God said to them, 'Be fruitful and multiply, and fill the earth'" (Gen. 1:28). There are three things to note here. First, Adam and Eve were to produce children. Second, they were to fill the earth and the implication is that they would have passed this commission on to their children. In this sense, Adam was the first

---

[1] Meredith G. Kline, *Kingdom Prologue: Genesis Foundations for a Covenantal Worldview* (Overland Park, KS: Two Age Press, 2000), 62.

spokesman for God on the earth, the first prophet, the first human to speak to man on behalf of God. Third, Adam was told to subdue the earth. Genesis 1:28 says, "God blessed them; and God said to them, 'Be fruitful and multiply, and fill the earth, and subdue it…'"

Adam's calling was not limited to the garden of Eden. He was to subdue the earth and fill it with others like him–image-bearers who were sinless and who would be fruitful and multiply and fill the earth. Recall Isaiah 45:18, which says:

> For thus says the LORD, who created the heavens (He is the God who formed the earth and made it, He established it *and* did not create it a waste place, *but* formed it to be inhabited), "I am the LORD, and there is none else." (Isa. 45:18)

Adam was told to rule over other creatures.

Genesis 1:28 continues, "…rule over the fish of the sea and over the birds of the sky and over every living thing that moves on the earth." Adam was king of creation. Listen to Psalm 8:3-8.

> [3] When I consider Your heavens, the work of Your fingers, The moon and the stars, which You have ordained; [4] What is man that You take thought of him, And the son of man that You care for him? [5] Yet You have made him a little lower than God, And You crown him with glory and majesty! [6] You make him to rule over the works of Your hands; You have put all things under his feet, [7] All sheep and oxen, And also the beasts of the field, [8] The birds of the heavens and the fish of the sea, Whatever passes through the paths of the seas. [9] O LORD, our Lord, How majestic is Your name in all the earth!)."

Adam was formed of dust with the breath of life breathed into him.

"Then the LORD God formed man of dust from the ground, and breathed into his nostrils the breath of life; and man became a living being" (Gen. 2:7). Adam was comprised of a body and soul.

As a sinless image-bearer, comprised of body and soul, who was both a spokesman for God and a ruler, Adam was told to fill the earth with others like him.

Adam was the first son of God.

Luke 3:38 says, "...the son of Enosh, the son of Seth, the son of Adam, the son of God." Adam was God's sinless son, an image-bearer of God, called to be fruitful and multiply, fill the earth, and subdue it–starting in the garden of Eden.

Adam was made outside the garden, which was the earth's first temple, then put in it.

"The LORD God planted a garden toward the east, in Eden; and there He placed the man whom He had formed" (Gen. 2:8). Genesis 2:15 says, "Then the LORD God took the man and put him into the garden of Eden to cultivate it and keep it." This is very interesting. The garden was the place of God's special dwelling on the earth with man. It was in the garden that Adam and Eve "heard the sound of the LORD God walking..." (Gen. 3:8). G. K. Beale comments:

> The same Hebrew verbal form (stem) *mithallek*...used for God's 'walking back and forth' in the Garden (Gen. 3:8), also describes God's presence in the tabernacle (Lev. 26:12; Deut. 23:14[15]; 2 Sam. 7:6-7).[2]

God's walking in the garden indicates His special presence among men. In this sense, the garden of Eden was a temple, a special dwelling place of God on earth among men. The garden of Eden was the earth's first sanctuary.

Since this may be a new concept for some readers, it is important to consider this a bit further. Was the garden the earth's first temple? Was the garden a special dwelling place of God among men on the

---

[2] G. K. Beale, *The Temple and the Church's Mission: A biblical theology of the dwelling place of God* (Downers Grove, IL: InterVarsity Press, 2004), 66.

earth? The text of Genesis 2 and 3 does not use those words to describe the garden of Eden. But as we have already seen, it does utilize language used elsewhere in Scripture that describes God's presence in Israel's tabernacle. Does the Bible look back upon the garden of Eden and indicate that it was, in fact, a temple, a sanctuary, the first special dwelling place of God on earth among men? I think it does.

Consider Ezekiel 28:11-19, especially verses 13-14, 16, and 18.

[11] Again the word of the LORD came to me saying, [12] "Son of man, take up a lamentation over the king of Tyre and say to him, 'Thus says the Lord GOD, "You had the seal of perfection, Full of wisdom and perfect in beauty. [13] "You were in Eden, the garden of God; Every precious stone was your covering: The ruby, the topaz and the diamond; The beryl, the onyx and the jasper; The lapis lazuli, the turquoise and the emerald; And the gold, the workmanship of your settings and sockets, Was in you. On the day that you were created They were prepared. [14] "You were the anointed cherub who covers, And I placed you *there*. You were on the holy mountain of God; You walked in the midst of the stones of fire. [15] "You were blameless in your ways From the day you were created Until unrighteousness was found in you. [16] "By the abundance of your trade You were internally filled with violence, And you sinned; Therefore I have cast you as profane From the mountain of God. And I have destroyed you, O covering cherub, From the midst of the stones of fire. [17] "Your heart was lifted up because of your beauty; You corrupted your wisdom by reason of your splendor. I cast you to the ground; I put you before kings, That they may see you. [18] "By the multitude of your iniquities, In the unrighteousness of your trade You profaned your sanctuaries. Therefore I have brought fire from the midst of you; It has consumed you, And I have turned you to ashes on the earth In the eyes of all who see you. [19] "All who know you among the peoples Are appalled at you; You have become terrified And you will cease to be forever."'" (Ezek. 28:11-19)

Notice that verse 13 is speaking explicitly of Eden, "You were in Eden, the garden of God." Verses 14 and 16 call Eden "the holy mountain of God." We will see in the next chapter that "…from the beginning of the Bible, mountains are sites of transcendent spiritual experiences, encounters with God or appearances by God."[3] Beale says of mountains:

> The prophet Ezekiel portrays Eden on a mountain (Ezek. 28:14, 16). Israel's temple was on Mount Zion (e.g., Exod. 15:17), and the end-time temple was to be located on a mountain (Ezek. 40:2; 43:12; Rev. 21:10).[4]

Identifying Eden as "the holy mountain of God" indicates God's special presence among men on the earth. In verse 18, the prophet Ezekiel says, "You profaned your sanctuaries." Beale comments upon this passage as follows:

> ...it should not be unexpected to find that Ezekiel 28:13-14, 16, 18 refer to 'Eden, the garden of God...the holy mountain of God', and also alludes to it as containing 'sanctuaries', which elsewhere is a plural way of referring to Israel's tabernacle (Lev. 21:23) and temple (Ezek. 7:24; so also Jer. 51:51). The plural reference to the one temple probably arose because of the multiple sacred spaces or 'sanctuaries' within the temple complex (e.g., courtyard, holy place, holy of holies)... Ezekiel 28 is probably, therefore, the most explicit place anywhere in canonical literature where the Garden of Eden is called a temple."[5]

This is an important passage of Scripture because it identifies Eden as a temple, the first mountain of God in which He dwelled among men on the earth. Kline says, "Paradise was a sanctuary, a temple-garden. Agreeably, Ezekiel calls it "the garden of God" (28:13;31:8f.) and Isaiah, "the garden of the Lord" (51:3)."[6]

It is interesting that Christian commentators are not the only ones who argue that the garden of Eden was the first temple of God

---

[3] "Mountain" in Leland Ryken, James C. Wilhoit, Tremper Longman III, Editors, *Dictionary of Biblical Imagery* (Downers Grove, IL: InterVarstiy Press, 1998), 573.

[4] Beale, *Temple and the Church's Mission*, 73.

[5] Beale, *Temple and the Church's Mission*, 75-76.

[6] Kline, *Kingdom Prologue*, 48.

on the earth. There is extra-biblical evidence of the garden as a temple from early Jewish literature. Fesko says:

> Perhaps one of the earliest writings that identify the garden of Eden as a temple comes from the Jewish book of Jubilees (c. 75-50 B. C.): 'And he [Noah] knew that the garden of Eden was the holy of holies and the dwelling of the LORD.'"[7]

Beale notes that the Qumran community, an intertestamental group, identified "itself as the 'Temple of Adam…' and 'an Eden of glory [bearing] fruits [of life]'."[8]

Adam was made outside the garden-temple then placed in it. But what was he supposed to do in or with that temple? His commission was obviously vitally connected to the garden God put him in, though not limited to it. Remember, he was to fill the earth and subdue it (Gen. 1:28). So the garden of Eden was not the end; it was only the beginning. Adam was called as an image-bearer of God who was sinless to multiply, fill the earth, and subdue it. His calling was to extend the garden-temple throughout the entire earth. In effect, the whole earth was to be God's special dwelling place with man. Eden was a prototype of something much greater.

Adam was commanded to cultivate and keep the garden in obedience to God.

Genesis 2:15 says, "Then the LORD God took the man and put him into the garden of Eden to cultivate it and keep it." If the garden was a temple, then Adam was a priest who offered up his work to God. It is of interest to note that when Adam is exiled from the garden due to his sin, Moses tells us that "God sent him out from the garden of Eden, to cultivate [or "serve"] the ground from which he was taken" (Gen. 3:23; Remember that Adam was created outside the garden of Eden.). Then, in the next verse, God "stationed the cherubim and the

---

[7] Fesko, *Last Things First*, 74. Beale dates the book of Jubilees at 160 BC. Cf. Beale, *Temple and the Church's Mission*, 77.

[8] Beale, *Temple and the Church's Mission*, 78.

flaming sword which turned every direction to guard [or "keep"] the way to the tree of life" (Gen. 3:24). Notice that Adam was to "cultivate [or "serve"]" the ground and the cheribum were to "guard [or "keep"] the way to the tree of life." These are the same words used together in Genesis 2:15, which says, "Then the LORD God took the man and put him into the garden of Eden to cultivate it and keep it." What does it mean that Adam was to "cultivate and keep" the garden, especially if it was the earth's first temple?

It is very interesting to note that these two words, "cultivate" and "keep," are used together in other Old Testament texts to refer to the work of priests in connection with Israel's tabernacle and temple (Num. 3:7-8; 8:25-26; 18:5-6; 1 Chron. 23:32; Ezek. 44:14).[9] Listen to Beale again:

> Genesis 2:15 says God placed Adam in the Garden 'to cultivate (i.e., work] it and to keep it.' The two Hebrew words for 'cultivate and keep' are usually translated 'serve and guard [or keep]' elsewhere in the Old Testament. It is true that the Hebrew word usually translated 'cultivate' can refer to an agricultural task when used by itself... When, however, these two words...occur together in the Old Testament..., they refer either to Israelites 'serving' God and 'guarding [keeping]' God's word...or to priests who 'keep' the 'service' (or 'charge') of the tabernacle (see Num. 3:7-8; 8:25-26; 18:5-6; 1 Chr. 23:32; Ezek. 44:14).[10]

> ...the writer of Genesis 2 was portraying Adam against the later portrait of Israel's priests, and that he was the archetypical priest who served in and guarded (or 'took care of') God's first temple.[11]

Since the garden of Eden was a temple, Adam was not only the first prophet and human king of the earth, he was its first priest. But Adam sinned. Adam's sin, therefore, gets him kicked out of the first house of God among men on the earth.

---

[9] Cf. Beale, *Temple and the Church's Mission*, 67.
[10] Beale, *Temple and the Church's Mission*, 66-67.
[11] Beale, *Temple and the Church's Mission*, 68.

Adam was commanded by God not to eat from the tree of the knowledge of good and evil and threatened death if he did.

> [16] The LORD God commanded the man, saying, "From any tree of the garden you may eat freely; [17] but from the tree of the knowledge of good and evil you shall not eat, for in the day that you eat from it you will surely die." (Gen. 2:16-17)

Adam had the law written on his heart and a specific external command from God not to eat of a certain tree. This was Adam's test, a probation. Would he be an obedient priest in God's house? Commenting on this prohibition, Beale says:

> After telling Adam to 'cultivate' and 'guard/keep' in Genesis 2:15, God gives him a specific 'command' in verse 16. The notion of divine 'commanding'... or giving of 'commandments'... not untypically follows the word 'guard/keep'... elsewhere, and in 1 Kings 9:6, when both 'serving' and 'keeping' occur together, the idea of 'commandments to be kept' is in view. The 1 Kings passage is addressed to Solomon and his sons immediately after he had 'finished building the house of the Lord' (1 Kgs. 9:1): if they do 'not *keep* My commandments...and *serve* other gods...I will cut off Israel from the land...and the house [temple]...I will cast out of My sight' (1 Kgs. 9:6-7)... Hence, it follows naturally that after God puts Adam into the Garden for 'cultivating/serving and keeping/guarding' (v. 15) that in the very next verse God would command Adam to keep a commandment: 'and the LORD God commanded the man...' The first 'torah' was that 'From any tree of the Garden you may eat freely; but from the tree of the knowledge of good and evil you shall not eat, for in the day that you eat from it you shall surely die' (Gen. 2:16-17). Accordingly, Adam's disobedience, as Israel's, results in his being cut off from the sacred land of the Garden.[12]

---

[12] Beale, *Temple and the Church's Mission*, 68-69.

Adam was given a suitable helper to fulfill his mandate from God.

[18] Then the LORD God said, "It is not good for the man to be alone; I will make him a helper suitable for him." [19] Out of the ground the LORD God formed every beast of the field and every bird of the sky, and brought *them* to the man to see what he would call them; and whatever the man called a living creature, that was its name. [20] The man gave names to all the cattle, and to the birds of the sky, and to every beast of the field, but for Adam there was not found a helper suitable for him. [21] So the LORD God caused a deep sleep to fall upon the man, and he slept; then He took one of his ribs and closed up the flesh at that place. [22] The LORD God fashioned into a woman the rib which He had taken from the man, and brought her to the man. [23] The man said, "This is now bone of my bones, And flesh of my flesh; She shall be called Woman, Because she was taken out of Man." [24] For this reason a man shall leave his father and his mother, and be joined to his wife; and they shall become one flesh. [25] And the man and his wife were both naked and were not ashamed. (Gen. 2:18-25)

Eve was Adam's helper. She was suitable for him. Adam could not fulfill the mandate of Genesis 1:28 alone. He needed a suitable helper. Eve was that suitable helper.

Adam was placed in a covenantal relationship with God.

At Genesis 2:4, Moses goes from using the word *Elohim*, translated "God," to using "LORD God." The word "LORD" is *Yahweh*, the covenant name of God. This could well indicate the covenantal status of man at creation. Surely, ancient Hebrew readers or hearers would have noticed this change. This at least suggests that covenant and the creation of man go together.

The prophet Isaiah may help us here.

[5] The earth is also polluted by its inhabitants, for they transgressed laws, violated statutes, broke the everlasting covenant. [6] Therefore, a curse devours the earth, and those who live in it are held guilty.

> Therefore, the inhabitants of the earth are burned, and few men are
> left. (Isa. 24:5-6)

The curse which extends to the earth came about due to a violated
covenant. Since the earth was cursed due to Adam's sin as our
representative, Adam broke covenant with God in the garden of
Eden.

The prophet Hosea may help us further. In Hosea 6:7 Israel is
likened unto Adam. "But like Adam they have transgressed the
covenant; There they have dealt treacherously against Me" (Hos.
6:7). Both Adam and Israel broke a covenant imposed upon them by
God. Both disobeyed and violated a covenant. Both covenants were
conditional, requiring the obedience of those in the covenant to
enjoy the benefits of the covenant. Moses tells us, "…in the day that
you eat from it you will surely die" (Gen. 2:17; cf. Exod. 19:5-6 for
the conditional nature of the Mosaic Covenant).

These factors taken together argue that God brought Adam into a
covenantal relationship with Him at his creation. Adam's covenantal
relationship with God or his communion with God as a sinless
image-bearer depended upon his obedience to God's law. This is
what theologians call the covenant of works or obedience. It is
called this due to the fact that the covenant was conditioned on
Adam's obedience. The term "works" in the phrase "covenant of
works" is a synonym for obedience. It is a term that reflects
subsequent biblical reflection upon Adam's creational vocation
(Rom. 5:12-21). Romans 5:19 justifies this term, when it says, "For
as through the one man's *disobedience* the many were made sinners,
even so through the *obedience* of the One the many will be made
righteous" (emphases mine). The opposite of "disobedience" is
"obedience." A legitimate synonym for "obedience" is "works." The
term "works" is also a good choice of words because it contrasts
with "grace" and gift" in Romans 5:17. Paul says there:

> For if by the transgression of the one, death reigned through the
> one, much more those who receive the abundance of *grace* and of
> the *gift* of righteousness will reign in life through the One, Jesus
> Christ. (Rom. 5:17; emphases mine)

A sinless image-bearer was called by God to be fruitful and multiply, and fill the earth with others like him. He was to subdue the earth and rule over other creatures, starting in the garden of Eden and going out from there. He was made of body and soul outside the garden. He was put in the garden to begin the task assigned to him as a priest. He was given a law to obey and a helper to compliment him so he could fulfill his task. He was a son of God. He was a spokesman for God (i.e., a prophet) and a ruler (i.e., king). He was in covenant with God. But he violated God's covenant. He sinned. He transgressed God's law. He was subsequently cursed, clothed with animal skins, then exiled from the garden at its eastern edge (Gen. 3:8-24). In essence, Adam got kicked out of God's house. Now he's sinful, is a terrible image of God, a covenant breaker, and no longer the keeper of God's garden-temple. What will God do now?

God's Remedy for Adam's Failure

According to Genesis 3:15, a seed or offspring of the woman will come to destroy the effects of the devil's work on the earth. "And I will put enmity Between you and the woman, And between your seed and her seed; He shall bruise you on the head, And you shall bruise him on the heel." First John 3:8 echoes this text, saying, "The Son of God appeared for this purpose, to destroy the works of the devil." Hebrews 2:14-16 is also instructive and illuminating at this point:

> [14] Therefore, since the children share in flesh and blood, He Himself likewise also partook of the same, that through death He might render powerless him who had the power of death, that is, the devil, [15] and might free those who through fear of death were subject to slavery all their lives. [16] For assuredly He does not give help to angels, but He gives help to the descendant of Abraham. (Heb. 2:14-16)

This seed of the woman will be a man–body and soul–an image-bearer of God. Listen to Galatians 4:4, "But when the fullness of the time came, God sent forth His Son, born of a woman..." Hebrews 2:14 says, "since the children share in flesh and blood, He Himself likewise also partook of the same." Colossians 1:15 says, "He is the image of the invisible God." The seed of the woman is the Son of God incarnate.

The seed of the woman is a sinless image-bearer. Hebrews 4:15 says, "For we do not have a high priest who cannot sympathize with our weaknesses, but One who has been tempted in all things as *we are, yet* without sin."

The seed of the woman has authority to rule over all things. Matthew 28:18 says, "And Jesus came up and spoke to them, saying, "All authority has been given to Me in heaven and on earth." Hebrews 1:3 says:

> And He is the radiance of His glory and the exact representation of His nature, and upholds all things by the word of His power. When He had made purification of sins, He sat down at the right hand of the Majesty on high. (Heb. 1:3)

The seed of the woman is the last Adam. First Corinthians 15:45 says, "So also it is written, "The first MAN, Adam, BECAME A LIVING SOUL." The last Adam *became* a life-giving spirit." The last Adam is the Lord Jesus Christ, the Son of God become man.

The last Adam, unlike the first, was tempted in the wilderness by the devil and did not succumb to temptation. Luke 4:1-2 says:

> [1] Jesus, full of the Holy Spirit, returned from the Jordan and was led around by the Spirit in the wilderness [2] for forty days, being tempted by the devil. And He ate nothing during those days, and when they had ended, He became hungry. (Luke 4:1-2)

The first Adam was a failure. He failed to subdue the devil in the garden. The last Adam is our hero.

The last Adam is the temple of God. He dwelt among us (John 1:14). Listen to John 2:13-22.

[13] The Passover of the Jews was near, and Jesus went up to Jerusalem. [14] And He found in the temple those who were selling oxen and sheep and doves, and the money changers seated *at their tables.* [15] And He made a scourge of cords, and drove *them* all out of the temple, with the sheep and the oxen; and He poured out the coins of the money changers and overturned their tables; [16] and to those who were selling the doves He said, "Take these things away; stop making My Father's house a place of business." [17] His disciples remembered that it was written, "ZEAL FOR YOUR HOUSE WILL CONSUME ME." [18] The Jews then said to Him, "What sign do You show us as your authority for doing these things?" [19] Jesus answered them, "Destroy this temple, and in three days I will raise it up." [20] The Jews then said, "It took forty-six years to build this temple, and will You raise it up in three days?" [21] But He was speaking of the temple of His body. [22] So when He was raised from the dead, His disciples remembered that He said this; and they believed the Scripture and the word which Jesus had spoken. (John 2:13-22)

Jesus' claim is that He will build a new temple. Note that after His resurrection, "His disciples remembered that He said this; and they believed the Scripture and the word which Jesus had spoken" (John 2:22). John makes a distinction between "the Scripture and the word which Jesus had spoken." The Scripture refers to the Old Testament. Thus, what John is saying is that the disciples, upon the resurrection of Christ, understood what Jesus said to be in line with the Old Testament. Jesus is the new temple promised in the Old Testament.

But our Lord Jesus Christ also creates a new temple called the church.

[16] Do you not know that you are a temple of God and *that* the Spirit of God dwells in you? [17] If any man destroys the temple of God, God will destroy him, for the temple of God is holy, and that is what you are. (1Cor. 3:16-17)

Ephesians 2:21-22 says:

²¹ in whom the whole building, being fitted together, is growing into a holy temple in the Lord, ²² in whom you also are being built together into a dwelling of God in the Spirit. (Eph. 2:21-22)

Paul is speaking about the church. The church is "a holy temple" and "a dwelling of God in the Spirit."

The last Adam was an obedient priest (Heb. 5:9-10) who creates a new priesthood for the house of God, which is the church of the living God. First Timothy 3:15 says, "*I write* so that you will know how one ought to conduct himself in the household of God, which is the church of the living God, the pillar and support of the truth." The church is now the house of God. First Peter 2:5 says, "you also, as living stones, are being built up as a spiritual house for a holy priesthood, to offer up spiritual sacrifices acceptable to God through Jesus Christ." Christ's church consists of priests offering up spiritual sacrifices.

The last Adam has a bride who assists Him in His task. Revelation 21:9 says,

> Then one of the seven angels who had the seven bowls full of the seven last plagues came and spoke with me, saying, "Come here, I will show you the bride, the wife of the Lamb; (Rev. 21:9)

The bride, the wife of the Lamb, is the church.

The commission by Christ to the apostles contained in Matthew 28:19-20 says:

> ¹⁹ "Go therefore and make disciples of all the nations, baptizing them in the name of the Father and the Son and the Holy Spirit, ²⁰ teaching them to observe all that I commanded you; and lo, I am with you always, even to the end of the age." (Matt. 28:19-20)

The apostles took this commission and preached the gospel, made disciples, then formed them into churches, thus extending the new temple inaugurated by Jesus Christ.

Ephesians 5:31-32 says:

[31] FOR THIS REASON A MAN SHALL LEAVE HIS FATHER AND MOTHER AND SHALL BE JOINED TO HIS WIFE, AND THE TWO SHALL BECOME ONE FLESH. [32] This mystery is great; but I am speaking with reference to Christ and the church. (Eph. 5:31-32)

The church is the wife of Christ who assists Him in His temple-building task all around the world.

Unlike the first Adam who disobeyed and caused death, the last Adam came to obey and to die that others might live. Romans 5:17 says, "For if by the transgression of the one [i.e., Adam], death reigned through the one, much more those who receive the abundance of grace and of the gift of righteousness will reign in life through the One, Jesus Christ." Adam failed to reign. Believers in Christ reign with Him now (Eph. 2:6) and will so forever.

Unlike the first Adam, the last Adam brings many sons to glory. Hebrews 2:10 says, "For it was fitting for Him, for whom are all things, and through whom are all things, in bringing many sons to glory, to perfect the author of their salvation through sufferings." This Adam failed to do because of his sin. Adam sinned and, thus, "fell short of the glory of God" (Rom. 3:23). Jesus suffered and then entered into His glory, as we have noted above. Whereas Adam's disobedience prohibited him from entering into glory, Christ's obedience is the ground upon which His children enter into glory.

Jesus Christ, the eternal Son of God become man, is God's remedy for Adam's failure. Jesus Christ takes His seed where Adam failed to take his. Salvation in Christ is better than creation in the image of God and citizenship in the garden of Eden. God does not place believers in Christ back at the starting line in the same position in which Adam was created. He grants irrevocable, eternal life based on the doing and dying of Jesus to all who believe the gospel. The end is the beginning glorified. It is better than the beginning. Christ takes all sinners who believe the gospel to His land, His eschatological temple, His paradise–the new heavens and the new earth, wherein dwells only righteousness. Praise God–Father, Son, and Holy Ghost. Amen!

Chapter 10

The Sabbath Rest of Creation (I):
Creation's coronation and goal

[1] Thus the heavens and the earth were completed, and all their hosts. [2] By the seventh day God completed His work which He had done, and He rested on the seventh day from all His work which He had done. [3] Then God blessed the seventh day and sanctified it, because in it He rested from all His work which God had created and made. (Gen. 2:1-3)

Introduction

This is a massive subject. The issue of the Sabbath has caused much ink to be spilled in our day as well as in previous days. Sabbath simply means *rest*. But what does God's rest mean for God and for us? There is much confusion on this issue due to not understanding the first revelation of the Sabbath as found in Genesis 2:1-3. This confusion, in part, is due to not allowing other parts of the Bible to explain the function of the Creator's Sabbath. In order to understand the Bible correctly, we have to understand what the Creator's Sabbath means, not only for us but for God. In order to do that, we have to let the Creator tell us what it means. He does just that in various places in the rest of Scripture.

Every picture tells a story and every person has a story. But there is one Person whose story stands apart from all others and that story is God's, recorded for us in the Bible. God's story tells us *that* He created, *what* He created in the first place, *why* He created man and *what* man's supposed to do, *why* there's so much trouble on the earth, and *where* history is heading. In the next two chapters, I want to show that understanding the Creator's Sabbath helps us understand the entire Bible–what it is about, what went wrong, how God's going about fixing what went wrong, and where history is heading. In order to do that, it is important to understand the Bible's diversity and unity and its beginning and end.

The Bible's Diversity

The Bible is a huge book with many diverse parts. We have both an Old and a New Testament. There are thirty-nine books in the Old Testament, written over a period of about 1,500 years by many different authors in different cultural and religious circumstances from which we live. The New Testament has twenty-seven books, written within the time-frame of one generation, a little over 2,000 years ago. But that generation existed in a world different than ours as well. Add to that the fact that the Bible has different kinds of literature, like narratives that tell stories of ancient events, people, and places, prophecies that tell of things to come, and epistles, which are letters written by apostles to local churches in the first century, and the Bible gives the appearance of being made up of disconnected books, written by various authors who did not know each other, over a long period of time with no central point, no plot, no story-line, and no conclusion.

The Bible's Unity

Those who read and think deeply upon the text of Holy Scripture realize that though it has diverse books and diverse authors and even diverse languages,[1] in all its diversity there is a wonderful unity in it. This unity is due to its divine author, who is none other than God Himself.

One of the ways the overall unity of the Bible may be seen is by comparing the beginning of the Bible with its end. I have a book on one of my shelves entitled, *The End of the Beginning: Revelation 21-22 and the Old Testament*.[2] The author, William J. Dumbrell,

---

[1] The Old Testament was written in Hebrew and the New Testament in Greek.

[2] William J. Dumbrell, *The End of the Beginning: Revelation 21-22 and the Old Testament* (Eugene, OR: Wipf and Stock Publishers, 2001; previously published by Baker Book House, 1985).

argues that the end of the Bible is the beginning of the Bible brought to its intended goal. He argues that the end is actually better than the beginning. Another author, T. D. Alexander, says:

> As is often the case, a story's conclusion provides a good guide to the themes and ideas dominant throughout. By resolving an intricate plot that runs throughout a story, a good denouement[3] sheds light on the entire story.[4]

This is true in a good mystery novel or movie. The plot (or riddle or problem to be solved) is revealed early on and is finally solved at the end and then everything in between makes more sense. But suppose you start a movie, then 15 minutes later someone walks in and begins to watch. They will have many questions. Though you might be hooked by then, the person who came late will not understand the plot, or setting, or background of the story. By the middle of the movie you will be putting clues together trying to solve the riddle. The other person will be asking you either to explain the various scenes, start the whole thing over, or they will leave. As well, there is usually a twist or twists in the story that finally ends in an amazing way that far exceeds your initial thoughts. The end ties up the loose ends of the beginning and middle and makes sense of the whole. So it goes with the Bible.

Commenting on the relationship between the beginning and end of the Bible Alexander says:

> The very strong links between Genesis 1-3 [the first three chapters of the Bible] and Revelation 20-22 [the last three chapters of the Bible] suggest that these passages frame the entire biblical meta-story.[5]

---

[3] A denouement is the final resolution of a plot, as in a drama or novel, a solution, or the end of a story that ties together its various parts.

[4] T. Desmond Alexander, *From Eden to the New Jerusalem: An Introduction to Biblical Theology* (Grand Rapids: Kregel Academic & Professional, 2008), 10.

[5] Alexander, *From Eden to the New Jerusalem*, 10.

A meta-story is the overarching story that all the parts of a book are serving. What are some of those themes that end up being in both the beginning and the end of the Bible? Let us explore a proposed answer to this question.

Seven Observations Tying the End of the Bible with the Beginning of the Bible

In this section, I want to explore some themes that occur at the end of the Bible which find their origin in the beginning of the Bible. This will help us see the big-picture so as not to lose the forest for the trees. It also will set a proper context for understanding the Creator's Sabbath—what it means for God and us.

The devil, who first appears in Genesis 3, ends up thrown into the lake of fire.

Revelation 20:7-10 says:

> [7] When the thousand years are completed, Satan will be released from his prison, [8] and will come out to deceive the nations which are in the four corners of the earth, Gog and Magog, to gather them together for the war; the number of them is like the sand of the seashore. [9] And they came up on the broad plain of the earth and surrounded the camp of the saints and the beloved city, and fire came down from heaven and devoured them. [10] And the devil who deceived them was thrown into the lake of fire and brimstone, where the beast and the false prophet are also; and they will be tormented day and night forever and ever. (Rev. 20:7-10)

The Bible has threads within it that deal with the effects of the devil's activity, not only in the garden of Eden but afterward as well. There is conflict between the woman's seed and the devil's seed throughout—the people of God and the children of the devil.

The first heavens and first earth of Genesis 1:1 become a new heaven and a new earth.

Revelation 21:1 says, "Then I saw a new heaven and a new earth; for the first heaven and the first earth passed away, and there is no longer *any* sea." Peter tells us that in this new heaven and earth "...righteousness dwells" (2 Pet. 3:13). Remember, God kicked Adam and Even out of the garden because they became unrighteous.

The tree of life, first revealed in Genesis 2, ends up on the new earth.

Describing the eternal state, Revelation 22:2 says, "On either side of the river was the tree of life..." Revelation 22:14 adds, "Blessed are those who wash their robes, so that they may have the right to the tree of life, and may enter by the gates into the city." The eschatological city, the new earth, contains the tree of life, which first appears in the Bible in Genesis 2:9.

God will dwell among all the citizens of the new earth.

Revelation 21:3 says, "And I heard a loud voice from the throne, saying, 'Behold, the tabernacle of God is among men, and He will dwell among them, and they shall be His people, and God Himself will be among them.'" God dwelt in the garden with Adam and Eve but they were exiled from that first dwelling place of God among men because of their sin. Then God dwelt in Israel's tabernacle and temple, then in Jesus Christ, as John tells us in John 1:14, "And the Word became flesh and dwelt among us..." God's dwelling with men is now experienced by the church, the new temple of God, the new house of God, which is "...a dwelling of God in the Spirit" (Eph 2:22). But in the new earth, God will dwell with everyone, not just the church in distinction from the outer world of men. The whole earth will be a special dwelling place of God among men.

There will no longer be any death in the new earth.

Revelation 21:4 says, "...there will no longer be any death." Death came when sin came way back in Genesis 3. In the new earth, there will no longer be any death.

The new Jerusalem is described with the symbolic language often used of temples.

Here is Revelation 21:10-22.

> [10] And he carried me away in the Spirit to a great and high mountain, and showed me the holy city, Jerusalem, coming down out of heaven from God, [11] having the glory of God. Her brilliance was like a very costly stone, as a stone of crystal-clear jasper. [12] It had a great and high wall, with twelve gates, and at the gates twelve angels; and names *were* written on them, which are *the names* of the twelve tribes of the sons of Israel. [13] *There were* three gates on the east and three gates on the north and three gates on the south and three gates on the west. [14] And the wall of the city had twelve foundation stones, and on them *were* the twelve names of the twelve apostles of the Lamb. [15] The one who spoke with me had a gold measuring rod to measure the city, and its gates and its wall. [16] The city is laid out as a square, and its length is as great as the width; and he measured the city with the rod, fifteen hundred miles; its length and width and height are equal. [17] And he measured its wall, seventy-two yards, *according to* human measurements, which are *also* angelic *measurements*. [18] The material of the wall was jasper; and the city was pure gold, like clear glass. [19] The foundation stones of the city wall were adorned with every kind of precious stone. The first foundation stone was jasper; the second, sapphire; the third, chalcedony; the fourth, emerald; [20] the fifth, sardonyx; the sixth, sardius; the seventh, chrysolite; the eighth, beryl; the ninth, topaz; the tenth, chrysoprase; the eleventh, jacinth; the twelfth, amethyst. [21] And the twelve gates were twelve pearls; each one of the gates was a single pearl. And the street of the city was pure gold, like transparent glass. [22] I saw no temple in it, for the Lord God the Almighty and the Lamb are its temple. (Rev. 21:10-22)

Eschatological or new Jerusalem is described as a cubed city of pure gold. Listen to Revelation 21:16-18 again.

> [16] The city is laid out as a square, and its length is as great as the width; and he measured the city with the rod, fifteen hundred miles; its length and width and height are equal. [17] And he measured its wall, seventy-two yards, *according to* human measurements, which are *also* angelic *measurements.* [18] The material of the wall was jasper; and the city was pure gold, like clear glass. (Rev. 21:16-18)

The only other golden cube in the Bible is the inner sanctuary of Israel's temple, called the holy of holies, the special dwelling place of God with man. Listen to 1 Kings 6:20, "The inner sanctuary *was* twenty cubits in length, twenty cubits in width, and twenty cubits in height, and he overlaid it with pure gold." Also, gold is often linked with the special dwelling place of God among men. Listen to Genesis 2:10-12.

> [10] Now a river flowed out of Eden to water the garden; and from there it divided and became four rivers. [11] The name of the first is Pishon; it flows around the whole land of Havilah, where there is gold. [12] The gold of that land is good; the bdellium and the onyx stone are there. (Gen. 2:10-12)

It is important to note that in Revelation 22:1 John was shown "a river of the water of life...flowing from the throne of God and from the Lamb." The entire new Jerusalem appears to be an expanded holy of holies–the special dwelling place of God among men.

One more observation on rivers in light of Revelation 22:1 may help. Rivers flow downhill. Since this is so, the rivers of Eden (Gen. 2:10-12) flowed downhill, which puts it uphill or upon a mountain. Now listen to Revelation 21:10-11a and 22:1, "And he carried me away in the Spirit to a great and high mountain, and showed me the holy city, Jerusalem, coming down out of heaven from God, having the glory of God" and "Then he showed me a river of the water of life..." Do you see it? The new Jerusalem is pictured as having a river flowing out of it and connected to a high mountain. The special dwelling place of God among men in the end of the Bible depicts a river of life and a high mountain. Where did this type of language and these concepts come from? From the Bible itself. The entry for "Mountain" in the *Dictionary of Biblical Imagery* reads:

> Almost from the beginning of the Bible, mountains are sites of transcendent spiritual experiences, encounters with God or appearances by God. Ezekiel 28:13-15 places the *Garden of Eden on a mountain. *Abraham shows his willingness to sacrifice Isaac and then encounters God on a mountain (Gen 22:1-14). God appears to Moses and speaks from the *burning bush on "Horeb the mountain of God" (Ex 3:1-2 NRSV), and he encounters Elijah on the same site (1 Kings 19:8-18). Most impressive of all is the experience of the Israelites at Mt. *Sinai (Ex 19), which *Moses ascends in a *cloud to meet God.
>
> A similar picture emerges from the NT, where Jesus is associated with mountains. Jesus resorted to mountains to be alone (Jn 6:15), to *pray (Mt 14:23; Lk 6:12) and to teach his listeners (Mt 5:1; Mk 3:13). It was on a mountain that Jesus refuted Satan's temptation (Mt 4:8; Lk 4:5). He was also transfigured on a mountain (Mt 17:1-8; Mk 9:2-8; Lk 9:28-36), and he ascended into heaven from the Mount of Olives (Acts 1:10-12).[6]

Jesus also designated a mountain in Galilee from which He gave the Great Commission to the eleven in Matthew 28:16, "But the eleven disciples proceeded to Galilee, to the mountain which Jesus had designated." Jesus is both the tabernacle of God among men (John 1:14) and a temple (John 2:19-22) who builds the new temple (1 Corinthians 3:16-17; Ephesians 2:19-22), His body, the church. Hebrews 12:18-24 contrasts Mount Sinai and Mount Zion in the context of the transition from the Old Covenant to the New Covenant. God's people have gone from one mountain to another. Surely these mountains are symbols of the Old Covenant and the

---

[6] "Mountain" in Ryken, Wilhoit, Longman III, *Dictionary of Biblical Imagery*, 573.

New Covenant and have their foundation in the first mountain-temple, the garden of Eden.

The curse that was inflicted in Genesis 3 due to Adam's sin is no more.

Revelation 22:3 says, "There will no longer be any curse; and the throne of God and of the Lamb will be in it, and His bond-servants will serve Him." Due to not serving God, the curse came upon man and the earth. In the eternal state, "there will no longer be any curse."

Conclusion

The Bible ends "[w]ith [a] remarkable vision of God coming to dwell with humanity on a new earth."[7] But the Bible started with God in the midst of His people in the garden of Eden, on a mountain, with precious stones present, with water flowing out of it, and in a context where Adam, the first prophet-priest-king, was supposed to subdue the earth and fill it with other image-bearers who were like him (i.e., sinless sons of God). What happened? Sin happened.

How Does all this Relate to the Creator's Sabbath?

The connections between the end of the Bible and its beginning are very instructive for our study at this point.

The connections between the end of the Bible and its beginning set the broader, big-picture context in order that the details might be easier to understand.

When we know the end of the story, we may better know the beginning and everything in between. For example, at the end of the

---

[7] Alexander, *From Eden to the New Jerusalem*, 14.

Bible, the entire new earth is sacred space. God dwells with all those in that place. In the beginning of the Bible, the sacred space was limited to the garden of Eden. In the middle of the Bible we see altars, a tabernacle, Israel's temple, Christ Himself, and then the church as sacred space–where God dwells with man in a special, unique way. All of these things–the garden of Eden, altars, Israel's tabernacle and temple, Christ and His church–point forward. They are symbolic of God's special dwelling among men on the earth but also mini-glimpses of the future. One day the whole earth will be sacred space where God dwells with men. Stephen G. Dempster says of the Old Testament what is true of the entire Bible, "The goal of the canon is clearly the great house of God, which is as inclusive as the globe."[8] What was instituted in the garden and spoiled by sin ends up brought to completion by our Lord Jesus Christ.

The connections between the end of the Bible and its beginning put the Creator's Sabbath in the context of completed temple-building.

We will discuss this further in the next chapter, but for now remember that temples are where God dwells on earth among men. The first temple was the garden of Eden, the first high mountain of the earth, where God dwelled with Adam and Eve. The Creator's Sabbath comes after He made the earth; it comes after He completed the crafting of His temple.

The connections between the end of the Bible and its beginning instruct us that the Bible goes from what God intended in the beginning, which was not accomplished by the first Adam, to what God Himself accomplishes through the last Adam, our Lord Jesus Christ.

In other words, the end is better than the beginning. The Bible goes from old creation to new creation via redemption. It goes from a

---

[8] Stephen G. Dempster, *Dominion and dynasty: A theology of the Hebrew Bible* (Downers Grove, IL: InterVarsity Press, 2003, reprinted 2006), 227.

good creation made bad by Adam's sin to a new, perfected creation made so by Christ's obedience.

The connections between the end of the Bible and its beginning help us understand the gospel.

God takes it upon Himself to dwell among men as the man, Christ Jesus. He came to be the hero of redemption, to do what Adam failed to do, to bring many sons to glory through sinless obedience. Because of sin, the last Adam, the Lord Jesus Christ, came to die for the forgiveness of our sins and create a seed, or spiritual children, who one day will fill the new earth, and enjoy inviolable communion with God. What Adam brought upon us all (i.e., guilt), Christ absolves and what Adam failed to do, Christ does (i.e., He brings many sons to glory through obedience). This is the gospel.

Chapter 11

The Sabbath Rest of Creation (II):
Creation's coronation and goal

[1] Thus the heavens and the earth were completed, and all their hosts. [2] By the seventh day God completed His work which He had done, and He rested on the seventh day from all His work which He had done. [3] Then God blessed the seventh day and sanctified it, because in it He rested from all His work which God had created and made. (Gen. 2:1-3)

In the last chapter, we saw that the end of the Bible is like the beginning but much better. God brings history to a glorious goal–a new heaven and a new earth that will never be tainted by sin. We saw that what God originally intended for the earth ends up happening when all history is brought to its apex, its climax, at Christ's second coming. Once the judgment dust is cleared, there will be a new heaven and a new earth in which dwells righteousness. The whole earth will be a special dwelling place of God among men. The whole earth will be a temple in which God communes with man. This is the eternal state, the consummated state. There will be no sin, no sorrow, no tears, and no death.

We also saw that this future state of affairs was not plan B. God created Adam as an image-bearer in covenant with Him who had the responsibility to be fruitful and multiply and fill the earth with others like him. He started this task in the garden of Eden which, as we have seen, was the first special dwelling place of God among men on the earth, the earth's first temple. Adam was commissioned to expand that Edenic temple to the four corners of the earth. Though Adam sinned not long after he was created and failed his assignment, God has taken it upon Himself to insure that the earth is full of His glory and that that glory is enjoyed by an innumerable host of men and women. This He does through the mighty warrior, our Lord Jesus Christ. Not only that, but God will make the world-to-come even better than the first world. Not only will it be absent of sin, sin will no longer be possible.

All of this has come in the context of our discussion on the biblical doctrine of creation. We are heading toward the end of this book and are considering the Creator's Sabbath. As was argued above, the end of the Bible is the beginning of the Bible glorified. We looked at the book-ends of the Bible because understanding that the end is the beginning glorified helps one understand the Creator's Sabbath in Genesis 2:1-3, the seventh day of the earth's history.

In this chapter, we will consider the Creator's Sabbath under these headings: 1. The context of Genesis 2:1-3; 2. The elements of Genesis 2:1-3; and 3. The rest of the Bible on Genesis 2:1-3. My goal is to show you that the Creator's Sabbath is not only God's enthronement over the entire creation, but an invitation for Adam to be like God by building a temple then resting from temple-building work and entering God's own rest–a state of existence qualitatively better than Adam's created state. Hopefully, by the end of this chapter, you will be able to understand why these things are so.

The Context of Genesis 2:1-3

Chapter 1 of Genesis gives us a broad overview of the first six days of the creation week. Man takes center stage in 1:26ff. (and then especially in chapter 2) as the only effect of God's creative work made in His image. Man is unique. He was created in the image of God and is responsible to be like God.

Genesis 2:4ff. focuses on the apex, the pinnacle of all that was created–man in the image of God. Chapter 2:4ff. takes us back to the sixth day of creation. In 2:7 we are told that God formed Adam from the dust of the earth and breathed into him the breath of life and Adam became a living being. God made a garden and placed Adam in that garden to cultivate and keep it. We have seen that this is priestly language. Adam was a priest in the Eden-temple. In the midst of the garden were two sacred trees–the tree of life and the tree of the knowledge of good and evil. Out of Eden flowed a river.

Eden was on a mountain, called God's garden and mountain in Ezekiel 28. There were also precious stones in Eden. This is the language that is consistently applied by the Bible to other earthly sanctuaries–including the eternal state as depicted in Revelation 21-22. Many of these things end up being used to describe the new heavens and the new earth. The garden was a limited space on the earth in which Adam was in communion with God as a sinless image-bearer. The garden of Eden was God's special dwelling place on the earth among men. In that sense, it was the first temple on the earth and Adam was this world's first priest.

In chapter 3 of the book of Genesis we are given the horrible news that Adam failed his assignment. Not only did he not subdue the earth and fill it with others like him but, prior to bearing children, he sinned and brought a curse upon us all, as well as the earth itself. He took and ate of the forbidden tree. Adam never got farther than the garden in his creational vocation. He sinned in the Eden-paradise and, as a result, was exiled.

In order to understand the Creator's Sabbath, we must have a firm grasp upon the context in which it comes to us. God creates the earth and then rests. He ceases from His creative work and then enters another form of activity–resting.

The Elements of Genesis 2:1-3

Creation completed

There is a clear announcement that the work of creation was completed: "Thus the heavens and the earth were completed, and all their hosts. [2] By the seventh day God completed His work which He had done" (Gen. 2:1-2a). God took six days to create and then He went from creating to sustaining that which He had created. He went from the work of creation to the work of providence. But remember, God's work of creation entailed the building of a temple. Heaven is

His throne and the earth is His footstool (Isa. 66:1). God built a temple then God rested.[1]

God rested

There is an announcement that once God completed the work of creation He rested from that work: "and He rested on the seventh day from all His work which He had done" (Gen. 2:2). This rest is not to be thought of as necessary because God had become weary or tired like we do. God does not get exhausted. He does not need to be replenished with energy. He simply went from one activity to another. But what does it mean that God rested? Exodus 31:17 comments on this very text. Here's what Moses says there: "for in six days the LORD made heaven and earth, but on the seventh day He ceased *from labor*, and was refreshed." Again, it cannot be that resting and being refreshed are necessary because God was tired. Resting and being refreshed are somewhat opposite to working. If God's work was the work of a master temple-builder, then once He finished the work of temple-building He went from one activity to another. The earth had become His footstool. He went from *royal work* to *royal rest* as King of creation. He went from making the heavens and earth to a posture of enthronement over the sphere He created. Let me explain why I say this.

Temple and rest are connected in the Bible. For instance, consider Psalm 132:7-8 and 13-14.

> [7] Let us go into His dwelling place; Let us worship at His footstool. [8] Arise, O LORD, to Your *resting place* [emphasis mine], You and the ark of Your strength. (Psa. 132:7-8)

> [13] For the LORD has chosen Zion; He has desired it for His habitation. [14] "This is My *resting place* [emphasis mine] forever; Here I will dwell, for I have desired it. (Psa. 132:13-14)

---

[1] We will explore this more below.

God's resting place is the temple. There He dwells. There is His footstool, and His throne is in heaven.

Israel's temple was a replica of the original creation. Listen to 1 Chronicles 28:2.

> Then King David rose to his feet and said, "Listen to me, my brethren and my people; I *had* intended to build a *permanent* [emphasis mine] home for the ark of the covenant of the LORD and for the footstool of our God.' (1 Chron. 28:2)

This is the language of temple enthronement. David intended to build a temple, which is the place on earth where God dwells with men, a localized footstool for God, who is King over all.

Exodus 20:11 says:

> For in six days the LORD made the heavens and the earth, the sea and all that is in them, and *rested* [emphasis mine] on the seventh day; therefore the LORD blessed the sabbath day and made it holy. (Exod. 20:11)

Notice the word translated "rested." It is not the same Hebrew word Moses used in Genesis 2:2-3. There he used the word *shabath*. Here in Exodus 20:11 he uses a word that is built off the same root as the words translated "resting place" in Psalm 132:8 and 14 and "permanent" in 1 Chronicles 28:2. As Kline says, "The Scriptures in effect interpret God's Sabbath rest at the completion of his cosmic house as an enthronement...."[2] The words of Isaiah 66:1 may help at this point: "Heaven is My throne and the earth is My footstool. Where then is a house you could build for Me? And where is a place that I may rest?"

The Creator's Sabbath indicates the completion of the earth as God's temple and the announcement of His enthronement over it as King.

---

[2] Kline, *Kingdom Prologue*, 35.

Seventh day blessed and sanctified

There is an announcement that God blessed the seventh day and sanctified it, as well as a reason annexed to this blessing and sanctification: "Then God blessed the seventh day and sanctified it, because in it He rested from all His work which God had created and made." (Gen. 2:3). This is the only day that is said to be "blessed" and "sanctified." It is hereby set apart. It has a unique status and function. God did not do this out of felt-need or in order for Him to become complete. He did this for man, just as He took six days to create for man. The Creator's Sabbath is a teaching tool for us. It not only tells us something about what God did a long time ago (built a temple, then rested), but it is also a symbol of what could and will happen in the future for man. This rest of God is something man will one day enjoy. And this we know because the Bible tells us so, as we will see below.

The Bible on Genesis 2:1-3

There are three passages in the Bible that shed peculiar light upon Genesis 2:1-3.

Exodus 20:8-11

> [8] "Remember the sabbath day, to keep it holy. [9] "Six days you shall labor and do all your work, [10] but the seventh day is a sabbath of the LORD your God; *in it* you shall not do any work, you or your son or your daughter, your male or your female servant or your cattle or your sojourner who stays with you. [11] "For in six days the LORD made the heavens and the earth, the sea and all that is in them, and rested on the seventh day; therefore the LORD blessed the sabbath day and made it holy. (Exod. 20:8-11)

Here the Sabbath for Israel finds its basis in creation and the divine Exemplar–God. It is of interest to note verses 8 and 11. "Remember the sabbath day, to keep it holy" (Exod. 20:8) and "For in six days the LORD made the heavens and the earth, the sea and all that is in them, and rested on the seventh day; therefore the LORD blessed the Sabbath day and made it holy" (Exod. 20:11). When did God bless the Sabbath day and make it holy? When He "rested on the seventh day." A day consecrated by God for man did not begin at Sinai. The Sabbath predates both Sinai and Israel as God's Old Covenant nation. It is not unique to Israel; it is for man from the beginning. The Sabbath day derives its existence from God at the creation. It has meaning prior to its status as an ordinance for ancient Israel..Its consecration as a sacred day dates to Genesis 2 not Exodus 20.

Mark 2:27-28

> [27] Jesus said to them, "The Sabbath was made for man, and not man for the Sabbath. [28] "So the Son of Man is Lord even of the Sabbath." (Mark 2:27-28)

Here Jesus affirms that the Sabbath was made for man and not man for the Sabbath. Man came first, then Sabbath. He does not say that the Sabbath was made for the Jews, but for man. The making of Sabbath happened at the same time-frame of the making of man and not at the making of the nation of Israel. Sabbath predates Israel. God instituted a Sabbath for man the day after He made him, man's first full day of life on the earth. The Sabbath is not as old as the Jews; it is as old as mankind (or at least one day younger).

Hebrews 3:12-4:13

> [12] Take care, brethren, that there not be in any one of you an evil, unbelieving heart that falls away from the living God. [13] But encourage one another day after day, as long as it is *still* called "Today," so that none of you will be hardened by the deceitfulness of sin. [14] For we have become partakers of Christ, if we hold fast the beginning of our assurance firm until the end, [15] while it is said, "TODAY IF YOU HEAR HIS VOICE, DO NOT HARDEN YOUR HEARTS, AS WHEN THEY PROVOKED ME." [16] For who provoked *Him* when they had heard? Indeed, did not all those who came out of Egypt *led* by Moses? [17] And with whom was He angry for forty years? Was it not with those who sinned, whose

bodies fell in the wilderness? [18] And to whom did He swear that they would not enter His rest, but to those who were disobedient? [19] *So* we see that they were not able to enter because of unbelief. [1] Therefore, let us fear if, while a promise remains of entering His rest, any one of you may seem to have come short of it. [2] For indeed we have had good news preached to us, just as they also; but the word they heard did not profit them, because it was not united by faith in those who heard. [3] For we who have believed enter that rest, just as He has said, "AS I SWORE IN MY WRATH, THEY SHALL NOT ENTER MY REST," although His works were finished from the foundation of the world. [4] For He has said somewhere concerning the seventh *day*: "AND GOD RESTED ON THE SEVENTH DAY FROM ALL HIS WORKS"; [5] and again in this *passage*, "THEY SHALL NOT ENTER MY REST." [6] Therefore, since it remains for some to enter it, and those who formerly had good news preached to them failed to enter because of disobedience, [7] He again fixes a certain day, "Today," saying through David after so long a time just as has been said before, "TODAY IF YOU HEAR HIS VOICE, DO NOT HARDEN YOUR HEARTS." [8] For if Joshua had given them rest, He would not have spoken of another day after that. [9] So there remains a Sabbath rest for the people of God. [10] For the one who has entered His rest has himself also rested from his works, as God did from His. [11] Therefore let us be diligent to enter that rest, so that no one will fall, through *following* the same example of disobedience. [12] For the word of God is living and active and sharper than any two-edged sword, and piercing as far as the division of soul and spirit, of both joints and marrow, and able to judge the thoughts and intentions of the heart. [13] And there is no creature hidden from His sight, but all things are open and laid bare to the eyes of Him with whom we have to do. (Heb. 3:12-4:13)

Notice at 3:16-19 "His rest" refers to the Promised Land that a whole generation of Israelites failed to enter due to unbelief. Hebrews 4:1 says that "a promise remains of entering His rest" for those to whom this letter was written and they may make good on that promise if they believe. So the rest of Canaan was not an end in itself. It pointed beyond itself to a future rest called "His rest."

Notice the allusion to the initial creation at 4:3b. There is also a quotation of Genesis 2:2 in Hebrews 4:4. Notice the mention of God's rest in 4:5. Notice also an allusion to God's rest in 4:6. Hebrews 4:9 says that "a Sabbath rest" remains for the people of God. It is vital to note something here. The word in Hebrews 4:9, translated "Sabbath rest" in the NASB is a different Greek word translated "rest" throughout the passage. "His rest" and the "Sabbath rest" that remains for the people of God, though related, are not one and the same thing. One is a state of existence (i.e., "His rest"); the other is something we do (i.e., "a Sabbath rest"). One is a type of life to be enjoyed; the other is its memorial and emblem. Finally, there is the mention of "His rest" in 4:10 and 11.

R. L. Dabney's comments on Hebrews 4 may be of help at this juncture.

This verse [Heb. 4:9] (with its context, which must be carefully read) teaches that, as there remains to believers under the Christian dispensation a hope of an eternal rest, so there remains to us an earthly Sabbath to foreshadow it. The points to be noticed in the explanation of the chapter are: That God has an eternal spiritual rest; that he invited Old Testament believers to share it; that it is something higher than Israel's home in Canaan, because after Joshua had fully installed Israel in that rest, God's rest is still held up as something future. The seventh day (verse 4) was the memorial of God's rest, and was thus connected with it. It was under the old dispensation, as under the new, a spiritual *faith* which introduced into God's rest, and it was unbelief which excluded from it. But as God's rest was something higher than a home in Canaan, and was still offered in the ninety-fifth Psalm long after Joshua settled Israel in that rest, it follows (verse 9) that there still remains a sabbatism, or Sabbath-keeping, for God's people under the new dispensation; and hence (verse 11) we ought to seek to enter into that spiritual rest of God, which is by faith. Now, let it be noted that the word for God's "rest" throughout the passage is a different one from "Sabbath." But the apostle's inference is that because God still offers us his "rest" under the new dispensation, *there remaineth to us a Sabbath-keeping under this dispensation.* What does this mean? Is the sabbatism

identically our "rest" in faith? But the seventh day was not
identically that rest; it was the memorial and emblem of it. So now
sabbatism is the memorial and emblem of the rest. Because the
rest is ours, therefore the Sabbath-keeping is still ours; heaven and
its earthly type belong equally to both dispensations.[3]

A temporal, earthy symbol exists as long as the consummation of
rest is not enjoyed in its fullness.

The writer of Hebrews sees God's rest from the foundation of
the world not as inactivity, or only as God's enthronement over the
world. He sees it as pointing forward and as something for man to
enter. It is not only something that points to Christ and then is
swallowed up and ceases to exist once He comes to live, die, and be
raised from the dead. The author sees God's rest as a state of
existence that could be attained. He sees it as a present symbol of a
type of life man did not enjoy via creation but is brought to only by
redemption. He sees it as eschatological life for man. And he sees
Israel's rest in the land of Canaan as a type of this rest, pointing
forward just as God's rest from the foundation of the world did. The
Creator's Sabbath, therefore, points to the eternal state. The rest of
Canaan was a type of something yet future and much more
permanent and glorious. The present Sabbath rest for the people of
God (Heb. 4:9) is a memorial of God's creational rest, Christ's new-
creational rest and a weekly reminder that more rest is to come.

God's pattern of working then enthronement-rest was to be
followed by Adam. Just as God built the earth to be a temple in
which He would dwell with man, so Adam's calling was, as God's
vice-regent, to obey God by extending the garden temple-culture to
the ends of the earth, which God made to be inhabited by man. Or,
as G. K. Beale puts it:

Just as God had achieved heavenly rest after [creating] and
constructing the beginning of his creational temple, so Adam

---

[3] R. L. Dabney, *Discussions of Robert L. Dabney* (Reprint ed.; Edinburgh:
The Banner of Truth Trust, 1982), 1:535.

presumably would achieve unending rest after ...extending the boundaries of the glorious Eden temple around the entire earth.[4]

Obviously, it would have taken much more time for Adam than God took to create and sit enthroned. The pattern set by God, however, was the pattern for Adam. In effect, God is saying, "Be like Me. I made you in My image. I created the earth as a footstool for Me. Now I want you to share in My glory and populate the earth with sinless image-bearers with which I will dwell." Again, the assumption is that once Adam finished his task, he too would have entered the rest of God and would have been finally enthroned as vice-king of all creation. We may also infer that Adam and all others would have been exalted to a status better than their created status.

The Creator's Sabbath is a pledge, a symbol pointing to the eternal state. It is the goal of creation. It is where Adam never arrived and no one since has either, except our Lord Jesus Christ, who suffered and then entered into His glory (Luke 24:7, 26, 46; Acts 26:23; 1 Pet. 1:11), a glory all believers will one day share (2 Thess. 2:14).

Listen to these passages from the book of Hebrews.

[1] God, after He spoke long ago to the fathers in the prophets in many portions and in many ways, [2] in these last days has spoken to us in His Son, whom He appointed heir of all things, through whom also He made the world. [3] And He is the radiance of His glory and the exact representation of His nature, and upholds all things by the word of His power. When He had made purification of sins, He sat down at the right hand of the Majesty on high, [4] having become as much better than the angels, as He has inherited a more excellent name than they. (Heb. 1:1-4)

[5] For He did not subject to angels the world to come, concerning which we are speaking. [6] But one has testified somewhere, saying, "WHAT IS MAN, THAT YOU REMEMBER HIM? OR THE SON OF MAN, THAT YOU ARE CONCERNED ABOUT HIM?

---

[4] G. K. Beale, *A New Testament Biblical Theology: The Unfolding of the Old Testament in the New* (Grand Rapids: Baker Academic, 2011), 40.

[7] "YOU HAVE MADE HIM FOR A LITTLE WHILE LOWER THAN THE ANGELS; YOU HAVE CROWNED HIM WITH GLORY AND HONOR, AND HAVE APPOINTED HIM OVER THE WORKS OF YOUR HANDS; [8] YOU HAVE PUT ALL THINGS IN SUBJECTION UNDER HIS FEET." For in subjecting all things to him, He left nothing that is not subject to him. But now we do not yet see all things subjected to him. [9] But we do see Him who was made for a little while lower than the angels, *namely*, Jesus, because of the suffering of death crowned with glory and honor, so that by the grace of God He might taste death for everyone. [10] For it was fitting for Him, for whom are all things, and through whom are all things, in bringing many sons to glory, to perfect the author of their salvation through sufferings. [11] For both He who sanctifies and those who are sanctified are all from one *Father*; for which reason He is not ashamed to call them brethren, [12] saying, "I WILL PROCLAIM YOUR NAME TO MY BRETHREN, IN THE MIDST OF THE CONGREGATION I WILL SING YOUR PRAISE." [13] And again, "I WILL PUT MY TRUST IN HIM." And again, "BEHOLD, I AND THE CHILDREN WHOM GOD HAS GIVEN ME." [14] Therefore, since the children share in flesh and blood, He Himself likewise also partook of the same, that through death He might render powerless him who had the power of death, that is, the devil, [15] and might free those who through fear of death were subject to slavery all their lives. [16] For assuredly He does not give help to angels, but He gives help to the descendant of Abraham. [17] Therefore, He had to be made like His brethren in all things, so that He might become a merciful and faithful high priest in things pertaining to God, to make propitiation for the sins of the people. [18] For since He Himself was tempted in that which He has suffered, He is able to come to the aid of those who are tempted. (Heb. 2:5-18)

[1] Therefore, holy brethren, partakers of a heavenly calling, consider Jesus, the Apostle and High Priest of our confession; [2] He was faithful to Him who appointed Him, as Moses also was in all His house. [3] For He has been counted worthy of more glory than Moses, by just so much as the builder of the house has more honor than the house. [4] For every house is built by someone, but the builder of all things is God. [5] Now Moses was faithful in all His house as a servant, for a testimony of those things which were to

be spoken later; [6] but Christ *was faithful* as a Son over His house-- whose house we are, if we hold fast our confidence and the boast of our hope firm until the end. (Heb. 3:1-6)

[26] For it was fitting for us to have such a high priest, holy, innocent, undefiled, separated from sinners and exalted above the heavens; [27] who does not need daily, like those high priests, to offer up sacrifices, first for His own sins and then for the *sins* of the people, because this He did once for all when He offered up Himself. [28] For the Law appoints men as high priests who are weak, but the word of the oath, which came after the Law, *appoints* a Son, made perfect forever. [1] Now the main point in what has been said *is this*: we have such a high priest, who has taken His seat at the right hand of the throne of the Majesty in the heavens, [2] a minister in the sanctuary and in the true tabernacle, which the Lord pitched, not man. (Heb. 7:26-8:2)

[11] But when Christ appeared *as* a high priest of the good things to come, *He entered* through the greater and more perfect tabernacle, not made with hands, that is to say, not of this creation; [12] and not through the blood of goats and calves, but through His own blood, He entered the holy place once for all, having obtained eternal redemption. (Heb. 9:11-12)

[11] Every priest stands daily ministering and offering time after time the same sacrifices, which can never take away sins; [12] but He, having offered one sacrifice for sins for all time, SAT DOWN AT THE RIGHT HAND OF GOD, [13] waiting from that time onward UNTIL HIS ENEMIES BE MADE A FOOTSTOOL FOR HIS FEET. [14] For by one offering He has perfected for all time those who are sanctified. (Heb. 10:11-14)

[19] Therefore, brethren, since we have confidence to enter the holy place by the blood of Jesus, [20] by a new and living way which He inaugurated for us through the veil, that is, His flesh, [21] and since *we have* a great priest over the house of God, [22] let us draw near with a sincere heart in full assurance of faith, having our hearts sprinkled *clean* from an evil conscience and our bodies washed with pure water. [23] Let us hold fast the confession of our hope without wavering, for He who promised is faithful; [24] and let us

consider how to stimulate one another to love and good deeds, [25] not forsaking our own assembling together, as is the habit of some, but encouraging *one another*; and all the more as you see the day drawing near. (Heb. 10:19-25)

[8] By faith Abraham, when he was called, obeyed by going out to a place which he was to receive for an inheritance; and he went out, not knowing where he was going. [9] By faith he lived as an alien in the land of promise, as in a foreign *land*, dwelling in tents with Isaac and Jacob, fellow heirs of the same promise; [10] for he was looking for the city which has foundations, whose architect and builder is God. (Heb. 11:8-10)

[13] All these died in faith, without receiving the promises, but having seen them and having welcomed them from a distance, and having confessed that they were strangers and exiles on the earth. [14] For those who say such things make it clear that they are seeking a country of their own. [15] And indeed if they had been thinking of that *country* from which they went out, they would have had opportunity to return. [16] But as it is, they desire a better *country*, that is, a heavenly one. Therefore God is not ashamed to be called their God; for He has prepared a city for them. (Heb. 11:13-16)

Much of the language of the book of Hebrews goes back to the garden of Eden. The concepts started there and were developed over time through the patriarchs and the nation of Israel. But Jesus is the only one who ends up doing what Adam failed to do–obey God perfectly as a sinless representative of others and enter into glory, bringing many sons with Him. Jesus also takes care of the issue of sin Adam introduced to mankind. Jesus is our obedient Priest, who both deals with our sin and builds God's present temple, the church, as King. All authority has been given to Him both in heaven and on earth (Matt. 28:18). He is the exalted Priest-King over God's house, populating it with citizens by the power of the Spirit who brings the gospel to souls with illuminating and soul-transforming power. The end is better than the beginning, and it is that to which the beginning was intended to arrive at all along.

Chapter 12

Conclusion:
Better than the beginning

We have gone from the purpose of all things created to the end or goal to which all things are heading. The triune God–Father, Son, and Holy Spirit–made all things out of nothing, for His own glory, tilted toward the Son from the beginning. Creation tells of God's glory and testifies of His existence and some of His attributes. Creation *ex nihilo* was completed by God in six days to set an example for man, the apex of creation. God then rested, indicating that His work of creation was complete and that He was now enthroned over it. Man was stationed on the earth as God's vice-regent, and as a prophet and priest. He was created morally upright, with knowledge and righteousness, as well as the law written on his heart. He was placed in the garden of Eden to both cultivate and keep the first temple and to spread it throughout the earth. He was in covenant with God. Adam was a representative of others. He could attain to God's rest, provided that he obeyed, extending the culture of the garden of Eden to the four corners of the earth. But he failed his vocation. Adam sinned. He did not reach the goal set before him by the Creator's example. He was exiled from Eden and we now live outside of paradise.

We have seen that the end of the Bible is the beginning of the Bible brought to its intended goal. A world filled with sinless image-bearers in glorified human nature was the goal of creation, all for the glory of God. The special presence of God permanently manifested to man *imago Dei* was the end to which creation pointed. Salvation from sin and its consequences does not take us back where Adam and Eve began. It takes us to a state of existence where they were not at their creation. Human nature is not only repaired by God's grace through the work of the incarnate Son of God, Jesus Christ, it is brought to a place where it was created to arrive, but failed to do so by the sin of our first parents. The fall into sin affected every man and every woman. It brought human nature into a state of guilt, pollution, and condemnation. Every one of us is born into a condition of helplessness. We are not able to change the state of our souls. Adam's guilt is our guilt. Polluted human nature is ours as well. We all sin. We all fall short of the glory of God.

The Bible is a big book. It has many different parts written by many different authors over a long period of time. At first glance, it gives the appearance of being a book with many ancient stories that do not have much, if anything, to do with each other. Viewed from a horizontal, man-centered perspective, some have concluded that it is comprised of two histories of religion–the religion of ancient Israel and the religion of the early Christians. Those who do, see little or no common threads throughout. It is viewed as a testimony of ancient religious people, written by various authors with no central or unifying theme. It is viewed as man's book about two of the world's religions.

Our study has shown us otherwise, however. Though there is diversity in the Bible, there is an overall unity produced by its divine author, God. We have seen the overall unity of the Bible by comparing its end with its beginning. The end is the beginning glorified. The end is that to which the beginning was made to attain. But what about the middle? It has been shown above from the New Testament that Christ creates a new temple which ends up in the special presence of God in the eternal state. But the bulk of the Bible is contained in the Old Testament and revolves around ancient Israel, God's Old Covenant nation. How does ancient Israel fit within the story-line of that which has been presented in the previous chapters? The answer to that question would take a book-length response to do it justice. Let me point you to a few arguments which show some connection between Adam, Israel, and Jesus Christ. Dempster's words capture this well:

> ...when Jesus begins his ministry, he as the new Adam and the new Israel, succeeds where the old Adam and the old Israel failed

(Matt. 4:1-11). Hence he recapitulates in his life the history of Adam and Israel.[1]

Recall that Adam was the first son of God (Luke 3:38). He was in covenant with God, responsible to obey God in order to attain an inheritance that was not his by virtue of his created status. Obedience for Adam was the way of blessing. He was put in God's place, the garden of Eden, under God's rule. But Adam, the first son of God, failed. As with Adam, ancient Israel was God's son. Exodus 4:22-23 says:

> [22] "Then you shall say to Pharaoh, 'Thus says the LORD, "Israel is My son, My firstborn. [23] "So I said to you, 'Let My son go that he may serve Me'; but you have refused to let him go. Behold, I will kill your son, your firstborn.""" (Exod. 4:22-23)

Israel is called God's son, His firstborn. Israel was taken from bondage in Egypt and gloriously rescued by God's almighty hand. This is called the exodus by Bible scholars. Israel was rescued by God, being brought out of slavery. The exodus is viewed as the redemption of the Old Testament by the Old and New Testaments. Israel was both rescued by God and transferred to the promised land of Canaan. But Israel's subsequent history is fraught with disobedience and covenant-breaking. It got to the point where God exiled ancient Israel from the land. Just as Adam failed his conditional relationship with God, so it went with ancient Israel (Hos. 6:7). Israel, like Adam, broke the covenant God imposed upon her. According to the covenant stipulations God imposed upon Israel, if she was obedient (Exod. 19:5-6), she would have remained in God's favor. But Israel, like Adam, was unfaithful to the Lord. Just as Adam sinned away his privileges and potential blessings, so it went with Israel. God raised up the prophets to confront Israel and to remind her of His saving purposes for the earth. The Old Testament ends with many lose ends and the expectation of God's future work on the earth.

---

[1] Dempster, *Dominion and dynasty*, 232-33.

When Jesus comes on the biblical scene, He is presented to us on at least two levels. He is both faithful Adam (cf. Rom. 5:12-21; 1 Cor. 15:22 and 45) and faithful Israel. Christ as faithful Adam is agreed upon by most Christians. However, Christ as faithful Israel may be new to some readers. Let's explore this briefly.

In the New Testament, there are some parallels between ancient Israel and Jesus Christ that give warrant to the view that Jesus is faithful Israel whose obedience brings blessings to others. For example, in the Gospel of Matthew, like Israel, Jesus goes to Egypt and then is called out of Egypt. Listen to Matthew 2:13-15.

> [13] Now when they had gone, behold, an angel of the Lord appeared to Joseph in a dream and said, "Get up! Take the Child and His mother and flee to Egypt, and remain there until I tell you; for Herod is going to search for the Child to destroy Him." [14] So Joseph got up and took the Child and His mother while it was still night, and left for Egypt. [15] He remained there until the death of Herod. *This was* to fulfill what had been spoken by the Lord through the prophet: "OUT OF EGYPT I CALLED MY SON." (Matt. 2:13-15)

After Jesus' baptism (Matt. 3:13-17), He "was led up by the Spirit into the wilderness to be tempted by the devil" (Matt. 4:1). Matthew tells us that "after He had fasted forty days and forty nights" (Matt. 4:2), He was tempted. But unlike Adam in the garden and Israel in her wilderness wanderings between Egypt and Canaan, Jesus did not succumb to temptation and sin. Recall that Israel's wilderness wanderings occurred over a forty year period due to sin (cf. Num. 14, especially verses 31-35) and after she passed through the Red Sea waters (Exod. 14-15). Jesus, however, passed through the waters of baptism, was tempted after forty days of fasting, and did not sin.

Another example of the New Testament relating ancient Israel and Jesus Christ comes from the apostle Paul. It is agreed upon by most Bible scholars that the redemption of the Old Testament was Israel's exodus from Egyptian bondage, as stated above. God rescued Israel from Egyptian bondage. The Israelites were under a dark and oppressive Egyptian ruler and God Himself delivered them from bondage and took them to the Promised Land through the human leadership of Moses and then Joshua. In Colossians 1:12-15 there are some interesting echoes of the exodus in the words of the apostle Paul. Here's what he says there:

> [12] giving thanks to the Father, who has qualified us to share in the inheritance of the saints in Light. [13] For He rescued us from the domain of darkness, and transferred us to the kingdom of His beloved Son, [14] in whom we have redemption, the forgiveness of sins. [15] He is the image of the invisible God, the firstborn of all creation. (Col. 1:12-15)

The redemption of sinners by Jesus has some parallels with the redemption of Israel from Egyptian bondage. Just as the Israelites were in a dark and oppressive place, so sinners redeemed by Jesus were trapped in the domain of darkness. Just as God liberated Israel from bondage, so Christ liberates sinners from bondage. Just as God took the Israelites out of Egypt and gave them an inheritance–the Promised Land–, so God takes sinners out of the bondage of sin and qualifies them for a future inheritance. Just as God ruled over Israel, so God places believing sinners in the kingdom of His beloved Son to be ruled by Him.

There are other parallels from other New Testament themes. Just as Israel was given a memorial meal (i.e., the Passover) to remember her deliverance from bondage, so the church has been given a memorial meal (i.e., the Lord's Supper[2]) to remember her deliverance from bondage. And finally, just as Israel was given a memorial day to remember her deliverance (i.e., the Sabbath), so the church has been given a memorial day (i.e., the Lord's Day) to remember her deliverance. What the Old Testament typified in Israel (i.e., God's son and firstborn), finds its fulfillment in Jesus, God's faithful Son and firstborn, and His body, the church.

---

[2] See my forthcoming *The Lord's Supper as a Means of Grace: More than a Memory*, to be published by Christian Focus Publications, for my understanding of the Supper as a means of grace and not only a memorial meal.

Due to Christ's faithfulness, He obtains an eternal inheritance for all those He came to save, unlike Adam and Israel who were unfaithful. The New Testament interprets Christ's coming as the fulfillment of Israel's hopes (e.g., Luke 1:26-38, 46-55, 67-79; 2:25-38; Acts 26:19-23). The New Testament also understands the church as the fulfillment of the eschatological Israel of Old Testament prophecy (e.g., Acts 2:14-21; 15:13-21; 2 Cor. 6:14-7:1; Gal. 6:16; Eph. 2:11-22; Heb. 8:7-13). The Lord's servant, Jesus Christ, unlike Old Covenant Israel, was faithful and became a "light both to the *Jewish* people and to the Gentiles" (Acts 26:23), just as "the Prophets and Moses said was going to take place" (Acts 26:22).

Old Testament Israel was a means to an end. The end is not Palestine. The end is not an earthly, Jerusalem temple at which animal sacrifices are offered. Ancient Israel was chosen by God to be a means through which the last Adam would come. She was also a means through which His Person, His work, His people, and His kingdom were typified. Israel has connections with the first man, Adam, and the last Adam, Jesus Christ.

The Bible is God's book. It possesses a unity, a progress of thought, and a goal that only God could ensure. It is not a book containing fallible records of two of the world's most prominent religions. It is the infallible, written Word of God. It is God's record of how He will get glory for Himself through what He does through His Son, the Lord Jesus Christ.

The world in which we now live is fraught with trouble. The answer to all the failure in the world is not a political one. The answer is not a Christian America or any other country in the world. The answer is not to convince others that humanity has utopian potential. Since the problem involves sinful human nature and is not fixable by sinful human nature, the solution is not to be found in sinful human nature. The answer is found in the Bible alone, specifically in the gospel of the Lord Jesus Christ.

The gospel is news from God that He has devised a way to repair human nature and take all creation to a glorious end. That glorious end, the city of God, new Jerusalem, the eternal state, the new heavens and new earth, is better than the beginning. In the beginning, though the potential for what comes about at the end was present, it was never attained by Adam. In the end, however, something better (much better!) than the beginning is brought about through the obedience of Jesus Christ. John Owen's words are helpful at this point:

> Man, especially, was utterly lost, and came short of the glory of God, for which he was created, Rom. iii. 23. Here, now, doth the depth of the riches of the wisdom and knowledge of God open itself. A design in Christ shines out from his bosom, that was lodged there from eternity, to recover things to such an estate as shall be exceedingly to the advantage of his glory, infinitely above what at first appeared, and for the putting of sinners into inconceivably a better condition than they were in before the entrance of sin.[3]

According to Owen, the end is better than the beginning.

Jesus Christ suffered for our sins then was rewarded for His obedience by being raised from the dead and exalted to the right hand of God in heaven. He will come again. He will transform the bodies of believers into bodies like His and He will usher in a new heaven and a new earth. In that place, He will be the center of attention. That eternal place is better than the garden of Eden and Israel's land. Indeed, it may be called Emmanuel's land. Emmanuel means "God with us."

I will allow the lyrics of an old hymn the final word of this book. It captures much of what I have tried to say above. I hope you will experience its truths now and one day with me in that place which is better than the beginning.

1. The sands of time are sinking, The dawn of heaven breaks, The summer morn I've sighed for, The fair sweet morn awakes; Dark, dark hath been the mid-night, But day-spring is at hand, And glory, glory dwelleth, In Emmanuel's land.

---

[3] John Owen, *The Works of John Owen,* Volume II (Edinburgh, Scotland and Carlisle, PA: The Banner of Truth Trust, Reprinted 1990), 89.

2. The King there in his beauty Without a veil is seen; It were a well-spent journey Though sev'n deaths lay between: The Lamb with his fair army Doth on Mount Zion stand, And glory, glory dwelleth In Emmanuel's land.

3. O Christ, he is the fountain, the deep sweet well of love! The streams on earth I've tasted More deep I'll drink above: There to an ocean fulness His mercy doth expand, And glory, glory dwelleth In Emmanuel's land.

4. The bride eyes not her garment, But her dear bridegroom's face; I will not gaze at glory, But on my King of grace; Not at the crown he gifteth, But on his pierced hand: the Lamb is all the glory Of Emmanuel's land. Amen.[4]

---

[4] *Trinity Hymnal*, hymn #599.

Bibliography

Alexander, T. Desmond. *From Eden to the New Jerusalem: An Introduction to Biblical Theology*. Grand Rapids: Kregel Academic & Professional, 2008.

Barcellos, Richard C. *The Lord's Supper as a Means of Grace: More than a Memory*. Fearn, Ross-shire, Scotland, UK: Christian Focus Publications, forthcoming.

Bavinck, Herman. *Reformed Dogmatics: God and Creation*, II, translated by John Vriend. Grand Rapids: Baker Academic, 2008.

Beale, G. K. *A New Testament Biblical Theology: The Unfolding of the Old Testament in the New*. Grand Rapids: Baker Academic, 2011.

_____. *The Temple and the Church's Mission: A biblical theology of the dwelling place of God*. Downers Grove, IL: InterVarsity Press, 2004.

Berkhof, Louis. *Systematic Theology*. Reprinted, May 1986; Grand Rapids: Wm. B. Eerdmans Publishing Co., 1939, 1941.

Dabney, R. L. *Discussions of Robert L. Dabney*, Volume I. Reprint edition; Edinburgh: The Banner of Truth Trust, 1982.

Daniels, Richard W. *The Christology of John Owen*. Grand Rapids: Reformation Heritage Books, 2004.

Dempster, Stephen G. *Dominion and dynasty: A theology of the Hebrew Bible*. Downers Grove, IL: InterVarsity Press, 2003, Reprinted 2006.

Dumbrell, William J. *The End of the Beginning: Revelation 21-22 and the Old Testament*. Eugene, OR: Wipf and Stock Publishers, 2001; previously published by Baker Book House, 1985.

Eadie, John. *Colossians*. 1980 reprint; Klock & Klock, 1856.

Fesko, J. V. *Last Things First: Unlocking Genesis 1-3 with the Christ of Eschatology*. Geanies House, Fearn, Ross-shire, Scotland, UK: Christian Focus Publications, Mentor Imprint, 2007.

Hodge, Charles. *Romans*. Reprinted 1989; Edinburgh and Carlisle, PA: The Banner of Truth Trust, 1835.

Johnson, Phillip E. *Defeating Darwinism by Opening Minds*. Downers Grove, IL: InterVarsity Press, 1997.

Kelly, Douglas F. *Creation and Change: Genesis 1.1-2.4 in the Light of Changing Scientific Paradigms*. Geanies House, Fearn, Ross-shire, Scotland, UK: Mentor, 1997, re. 2010.

_____. *Systematic Theology, Volume One, Grounded in Holy Scripture and understood in the light of the Church, The God who is: the Holy Trinity*. Geanies House, Fearn, Ross-shire, Scotland, UK: Mentor, 2008.

Kline, Meredith G. *Kingdom Prologue: Genesis Foundations for a Covenantal Worldview*. Overland Park, KS: Two Age Press, 2000.

Muller, Richard A. *Dictionary of Latin and Greek Theological Terms*. Grand Rapids: Baker Book House, 1985, Second Printing, September 1986.

_____. *Post-Reformation Reformed Dogmatics: The Rise and Development of Reformed Orthodoxy, ca. 1520 to ca. 1725*,

Volume Two, Holy Scripture, The Cognitive Foundation of Theology. Grand Rapids: Baker Academic, 2003, Second Edition.

Owen, John. *Biblical Theology.* Pittsburgh: Soli Deo Gloria Publications, 1994.

_____. *The Works of John Owen,* Volume I. Edinburgh, Scotland and Carlisle, PA: The Banner of Truth Trust, reprinted 1987.

_____. *The Works of John Owen,* Volume II. Edinburgh, Scotland and Carlisle, PA: The Banner of Truth Trust, reprinted 1990.

Piper, John. *Let the Nations be Glad: The Supremacy of God in Missions.* Grand Rapids: Baker Books, 1993, sixth printing 1996.

Reymond, Robert L. *A New Systematic Theology of the Christian Faith.* Nashville: Thomas Nelson Publishers, 1998.

Ryken, Leland, Wilhoit, James C., Longman III, Tremper, Editors. *Dictionary of Biblical Imagery.* Downers Grove, IL: InterVarstiy Press, 1998.

Shaw, Robert. *An Exposition of the Westminster Confession of Faith.* Geanies House, Fearn, Ross-shire, Scotland, UK: Christian Focus Publications, 1998.

Smith, Morton H. *Systematic Theology,* Volume I. Greenville, SC: Greenville Seminary Press, 1994.

The Baptist Confession of Faith & The Baptist Catechism. Vestavia Hills, AL: Solid Ground Christian Books and Carlisle, PA:

Reformed Baptist Publications of the Association of Reformed Baptist Churches of America, 2010.

Trinity Hymnal: Baptist Edition. Suwanee, GA: Great Commission Publications, Inc., 1995.

Waldron, Samuel E. *A Modern Exposition of the 1689 Baptist Confession of Faith*. Reprinted 2005; Darlington, England: Evangelical Press, 1989.

Watson, Thomas. *A Body of Divinity: Contained in Sermons upon the Westminster Assembly's Catechism*. Edinburgh, Scotland and Carlisle, PA: The Banner of Truth Trust, 2000.

Scripture Index

Name and Subject Index

CPSIA information can be obtained at www.ICGtesting.com
Printed in the USA
BVOW08s1838070515

399219BV00009B/567/P